THE GIFT OF RHYME

VOL. I

I0134510

BY

STANLEY PITCHFORD

P.O. Box 2535
Florissant, Mo 63033

Edited by: Kendra Koger and Brenda Matthews

Cover Designed by Sheldon Mitchell of Majaluk

Manufactured in the United States of America

Library of Congress Control Number: 2010909489

ISBN: 978-0-9819913-6-8

For information regarding discounts for bulk purchases, please contact Prioritybooks Publications at +1 314 306 2972 or info@prioritybooks.com.

You can contact the author at: jabberstan@yahoo.com.

First Prioritybooks Printing: April 2010

Printed in the United States of America

Table Contents

THE GIFT OF RHYME

VOL. I

BY

STANLEY PITCHFORD

DEDICATION PAGE

First of all, I would like to thank God,
He spared me mercy and faith to get me past some odds.

Then I thank Susan Pitchford, my granny, a great wisdom teacher strong,
She gave me a lot of knowledge, so I express it in these poems.

These poems are dedicated to Damon and Reginald Pitchford

On my mother's side;
And I dedicate this to Jarron, Emory, Brandon, Jasmine and Brittany;
I am not going to forget you all alright.

And this one is for Mary Pitchford and Stanley Tilghman too,

Because if they had never met, these poems would not have made it to you;
This is also for Cassandra Howard, a "Big Momma" for real;

And these are for nieces Reje and Marciay, because I want them to be more successful than me.

And these rhymes are for Facebook and MySpace friends, who encouraged me so,

And now you got your wish and so you can enjoy my book of flows;

And I am sure I missed somebody so I dedicate this to you now;

As you read my lyrical potential, I hope it gives you a warm smile.

BE BLESSED

Whether times are good or bad, I WILL NEVER FORGET ABOUT GOD.

Introduction

Stanley Pitchford's book, "The Gift of Rhymes, Volume 1" is a collection of poems, rhymes, and spoken words that comes straight from his heart. Since we are in some very difficult times now, we tend to forget that we are witnesses, and were given mercy to make it another second, if we are alive. This book of poems explores love, because without charity, the whole world might be chaotic. Other topics include: rap, success and motivation, the economy, soft poems, math, rhymes for the lady, faith and much more. The purpose of this book is to give readers something to look at, take away or reflect on what matters in this life. There are so many topics and concepts discussed in this book that you are absolutely bound to enjoy something, if not all.

Are you ready for my lyrical style? Do you think I have what it takes lyrically? Do you think I am a better poet or author? Pick up this poetry book today and you can be the judge.

THE GIFT OF RHYME

VOL. I

BY

STANLEY PITCHFORD

Section One:
Love

CHASING LOVE

See, I got this crush,
It teases my emotions too much;
Thought I was in love, just a notion,
Going through the motions;
This girl was a good-looking dime on time,
I'll have her with wine;
Talk about her in my rhyme,
Make her feel so divine;

Her eyes shine like jewels,
But then again I must have been a fool;
I thought everything was cool,
Look at what chasing love, do to you;
Only chased love once,
It was no fun;
It was only a fling thing,
Nothing got done;

So now I'm thinking harder,
Critically smarter;
I choose to not get caught up,
The game well thought up;
I got to feel like an ocean floor,
Fresh, ready to explore;
Love can come and go,
Until you find the right flow;
Then you're thinking the rhythm strong,
It will last long;
Later on, there's nothing to condone,
When you're on your own;
Here I go chasing love,
When I really should be chasing God above.

What Kind of Love?

What kind of love is this?
For a second you lose your place on Earth;

Something must be going on in your heart and mind;
Priceless is what that lady must be worth;

To you she was sweet like a candy drop,
If you were sore she made you feel cotton soft;

I do not know what is going on but the feeling is hot,
Now you see what a true love can do;
When you want her and she wants you.

And it is the way she opens up her heart,
Like a door, wide open to you;

She makes you want to feel guilty at heart,
Her innermost emotions gently rest on you like grass and dew;

Really, what kind of love,
Have you got yourself into?

Sounds so romantic and poetic, sure enough,
She is so original, just for you.

Look At What Love Can Do

Is it really Love, or is it really Lust?
Is this really someone I am thinking of, either way, my heart is
going to bust?
She says we are going to be together,
Good or bad weather;
We are going to be scrubbing each other's back,
She keeps in touch with me to keep me and her on track;
She seems like she is cool,
I do not know what to do!
But she got some funny ways,
I cannot figure out, I still need to pray;
For me, she never went head over hills,
Never really told me how she feels;
I think saying things is one thing too,
But then it comes in what one will do;
See, I am just so confused,
This Love thing can give you the blues;
Then your emotions feel so used,
Leaving you soft like cotton, look at what Love can do;
I cannot take precautions,
Lost in my mind, I am noxious;
I tried to get on my knees,
I wished I could come to a decision, please!
My mind and heart synchronize,
I cannot lie.

Look at What Love Can Do   PART 2

I got soft on this girl like slush,
Why did I have this rush?
I got this amazing crush,
My heart pumping as such.
What is this I feel?
Got my heart locked hard like steel;
I just like how she do her thing,
She's like happiness to the blues I bring;
It's like I am addicted to her like a drug.
I need her, I cannot get enough;
I can see her as a friend and a lover too;
I cannot seem to hate her,
Look at what Love can do.
Now I must put her to the test still,
For me will she go head over hills?
Will she be my supportive leg,
Just in case I go over the edge?
I do not really know,
If she even likes the way I go;
But this strange thing called Love,
Got me still hanging with her tough;
But she wants us together,
But I am still going through stuff, a low budget fellow;
I still hold on strong,
I must get myself moving along;
It's so true,
How strange Love can do to you.

Look At What Love Can Do: Part 3

I got so many takers,
This girl wants me to be her maker;
She wants us to get things cooking,
I like my single life now, I like how I am looking;
Relationships are getting out of control,
So many bad baby mamma and baby daddy episodes;
At this moment drama is all I see,
For now I just got to worry about me;
I just show my own Love anyway I can,
Love between a man and woman is something I could never
understand;
This I cannot study or analyze,
You could be in a deep love and then get a big surprise;
You held up your end,
Thought she was more than a friend;
Now you're thinking this is foreplay
Even gave her a gift on Valentine's Day;

And all this stuff and other great things too,
And then all of that for nothing look at what Love can do;
She takes you for a ride,
But it was more like emotional homicide,
Now you must live your life,
And other trials to write;
I had to jot this down,
I just kept a frown.

Section Two:
Grace and Mercy

SEE, WE REALLY NEED A PEACE CALLING

See, we really need a peace calling
Because violence has gone astray
You cannot blame everything on the economy,
Some people just made struggles for themselves, okay;

And some was brought up wrong,
Street hustling is all they know;
They found violence as a means to get what they want
And that is the road they chose to go;
You see so much violence,
So many people are angry at man;
You can try to be positive yourself,
But some people just do not care right now in this land;

See, we have been preaching "STOP THE VIOLENCE" for years
But really, does it ever cease?
When we attend someone's funeral that is the only time
When they have true peace;

And praying to God is the only answer
While running this race;
And if we are breathing another second
I just thank God for His mercy and grace;

See, there have been so many mistakes made
So many lessons taught;
So many bad consequences for our choices
Because we've not done as we ought;

People are so violent,
Why is the innocent dying so young?
See, you're living life is not even a smidgen of
The great mercy God has spared for every one

So be thankful for this moment,
Because it might be the only good thing left;
Be grateful if it is just a cold,
Because others only got 24 seconds of breath;

Yet we need a peace calling,
Because times need to get better for real;
And even with that hope,
It would help to be sure of your place with God still;

And Prayer makes my day better
Because it makes me believe there is hope on the way;
And then we can enjoy ourselves in the light,
Get out these dark rainy days;
But in the midst of your bad day,
There is always joy now;
Because we all should be thankful
If we have the features of a smile;

But God takes us through each storm,
And our struggles are always underway;
And some people get insane and get violent
But they are the ones that should pray.

I wish we were an almost balanced nation,
But I must pray to feel better about hope in time;
It seems I look at the simpler things, like I was spared
Mercy I was able to get through this rhyme.

I Should Be On Bended Knees

I should be on bended knees,

Because I have made mistakes so;
Yet God has spared me mercy
So grateful to him for that though;

I know I will get some thunder,
Even get hit with heavy rain;
But if I got God in my heart,
I should not go insane;

The love from God will make you stronger,
He will sustain your resistance longer;
The only ticket is just to believe,
That Christ died for me and has faith and receives;

The sins I go through MY, MY, MY,
The struggles I face yet blessed if I still get by;
The drama feels heavy like boulders,
But if I am working through Christ, like Sisyphus, my mission is
not over;

I could be going through worst,
Yet thinking about Christ gives me joy;
I must think Christ first,
I do not mind being God's employed;

I should have been on my knees,
So many mistakes made, Jesus already paid the sin fees;
All that He paid for and He is so worthy,
I know I will always serve Him, and why should He serve me?

Only Christ is the true friend,
When that hurricane comes in tough times;

Nobody else can understand your personal rain,
I need Christ working my heart and mind;

God sends the right wisdom,
Allows the right trouble for you to understand;
He wanted you to see a particular storm,
So that you can rejoice in Him, hold to His hand;

See, I should always be on my knees,
Because my flesh steady tries to get in the way;
Trouble is never what I want or need
But adversity comes and I must pray;

But I will rejoice through my rain,
For which I have no control in this thing;
But then situations could be worse,
I should be saying LORD HAVE MERCY on me first;

Only through the wisdom and patience of God I get better,
I grow with God's plan altogether;
I am not supposed to see the faith,
I am not worthy to keep my own road straight;

I tried to plan my day,
But really, who said it was ever mine?
I wanted to do things one way,
But His way was better and it was on His time;

See, I should be on my knees,
He has more blessings than I have sins;
He will pinpoint your purpose in life,
But, with Christ, is where one must begin;

I need to get in His Word, it is no other reason,
Still keep praying without ceasing;
God has granted me grace, things I never thought I would see,

I am not sure if I was worthy of it, but it was spared for me.

What If You Only Had Mercy?

What if all you had was mercy and you had to give God praise?
You know how it can be, we could come to those days;
Do not look at me like I am stupid,
Even if times get tough, we still must show Genuine Love for God above.
I just want to thank God for the mercy,
See, I know about someone who is worthy;
You know I must give Him praise,
Took me through some challenging days;

I gloried in the good, struggled through the bad,
But if God still spared the mercy, why should I be sad?

See, I could be poor but others going through worst,
God does not have to tell me whom I should go to first;
It is just a blessing even if I am alive for real,
I must praise Him,
He allowed me breath to awake another day still;

He left me alive another morning,
Some go without a warning;
You never know the grind,
I must thank God for mercy and I must praise Him,
for that place I will be going in time;

Something About That Word Mercy

I know that so many things could go wrong,
But it is something about mercy that kept me going strong;
Struggles weigh like boulders,
But if I am able to shoot for victory through faith,
I am grateful if my life is not over,
I know someone knows what I am talking about,
Been through a rough day, thought mercy would not hold out;
You're already feeling bad, and then something happens worse;
See, even if the slightest thing happens I will always put God first;
I know who holds the mercy key and allowed me through the
joyful door;
Thankful if I am allowed another day and I am ready to explore,
I know that you heard me,
It is something about that word MERCY.

Thankful Because God Spared the Mercy

Only for God I know what I am after, because He spared me
mercy;
Because any day could be the final chapter, I know somebody
heard me;

I am glad I have a Savior, to guide me through the storms;
Disasters could disrupt my behavior, but knowing about God keeps
me out of harm;

See, times could be much worse, but God says hold on strong;
My faith in God should always be first; He is the reason why we
got to this day to carry on;
My finances may not be totally straight, but I am grateful if God
left me breathing;
And I must keep the faith, for that nice place I will go upon
leaving;

The hurricanes cannot scare me, if my faith in God is strong;
With God there is no worry, because His way is never wrong;
We know who has the answer; we have not praised Him enough;
He has moves better than disco dancers; He can pave the way
through the boulders and tumultuous stuff;

Disasters can come without warning, still thankful if I made it to
another morning;
He gave so many blessings, I went through so many lessons;
The journey through life is never easy, and I am not worthy for
Him to please me;
Just think about my many wrongs, but you know I had to go this
lyric strong!

I Made It Right Here

I made it right here, even though the road was rough;
Shed so many tears, and times were tough;
If I got another day and spared another breath,
Just so thankful if I got that left;
I made it right here, to read this rhyme,
Some people cannot breathe another second at this time;
I am guilty for being mad about who owes me what,
When I should be blessed and just keep my mouth shut;
I suffer and go through so much pain;
Never think to realize people living worse in the game;
So even when I complain, I know I am not alone;
This is why we all need faith to keep pulling on,
Even now I feel like shedding a tear;
The reason is that, I made it right here.

What Matters Is What Is Worse

Be thankful if you have a job, a roof over your head;
So many people lost their homes to flood, it seems like they got
robbed instead;
I thank God if it is just a pay cut, because I do not want the
severance pay,
And with things already expensive, still hard to make it any way;
And maybe your car was stolen, but at least you were not carjacked
and killed;
We just have to look at what matters is what is worse, for real
So much going on and this just has to be said;
So much drama will have you thinking foolish thoughts in your
head;
You just went through a quick storm,
But others may have a continuous hurricane;
It does not matter the struggle God will take all of us through
anything.

See, What If

See, what if you had no power, damaged was your land;
Your emotions bubbling for hours, no food in your hands?
A disaster may have happened, but thank God you're alive to
witness;
Because some people may have drowned,
got killed, or could not handle their business;
See, what if God's Mercy was not that strong?
What if a huge flood came through and took us all along?
We need to be thankful for what we have, no doubt,
Some living worse than me, so I know what I am talking about;
I am just scared of cold weather,
And someone is going through a hurricane;
Some people surviving the storm,
But those are the ones going insane;
See, I know something we should be blessed about, true,
We might have bad storms but some only have months stuck up in
ICU.

Section Three:
BLESSINGS

Anytime I Am Alive, It Is a Blessing

I learned so many lessons,
Anytime I am alive it is a blessing;
I continue to help out my soldiers,
Bring the math lesson, it is not over;
Our future is on the rise,
Could take us by surprise;
All this technology out in the open,
The respectful view left soaking;
Get all you can, this is your token;
Do not get wrapped up in bad drama, because your life can be
broken;
Anytime you are alive, you are not finished;
I got to continue, until my style just diminishes;
I just keep thinking,
Fast like human eyes blinking;
I treat every move like it is one shot,
And this is all I got;
I want to settle for better than best,
But I will take nothing less;
I hate to live life stuck in a mess,
It brings on stress;
But I thank God for where ever I am at if I am alive;
Some died, yet I am still able to survive;
God is so gracious,
I am so blessed right now,
because of Him I got patience.

Just Forget About Your Bad Day,
When Someone Has It Worse

Just forget about your bad day, when someone going through
something worse;
It is just a blessing to be alive that is why I will always put God
first;
You might get the lightning, and someone else has the rain and the
hail,
Bad things are never exciting, but I would be blessed if I am still
alive to tell;
Some people could lose their homes with how the rain delivers,
Thankful if that flood never came my way, cresting high is the
Mississippi River;
We need to be blessed for wherever the gas is right now;
Because we could have some real bad times anyhow;
And as I keep living, I learned something so true;
You might think you are in hard times, but someone is always
worst off than you,
Thank God for the joy of the strong morning sun,
If I make it another day, then that is another blessing in life to carry
on.

Blessed For Another Moment

So much stuff has happened,
More than what I am rapping;
Blessed if I get through it,
God already knew it;
You can't ever call the shots,
Still blessed with what you got;
Sometimes it's hard to keep things holy,
All the filth before me;
Christ I pray just holds me,
Do not let Satan fold me;
It's so much in people's lives,
Plus we got to still try to survive;
Blessed if I get another breath,
So thankful if I got that left;
Love everyday with a struggle,
Because I know God still loves you;
I go through so much stress,
I need to get it off my chest;
I need to do my best,
I got to recognize the success;
The glory is not mine,
Only faith in God can be that fine;
I just thank Him if I am still breathing,
Thank Him for all achievements;
Been on Earth at least eleven thousand days,
Yet I must still give praise;
Some got problems worse in their lives,
You are blessed to get another day if you are alive!

Blessed For Another Moment Part 2

See, I do not know my own future,
Do not know how this life can do you;
I do not have to say it;
It is the present times we are in that will convey it;
You are just blessed with whatever,
I try to be clever;
You can try to be better,
But some things do not fold together;
I just think so much,
So many peoples' lives I have touched;
With this math it seems I'm preaching,
Trying to see how many I am reaching;
I still must live, its not over,
I got future youths looking over my shoulders;
I am just blessed for another moment,
God knows I would want it;
I just pray for a life I can feel,
Blessed to help out still;
It's all about motivation,
Plus God already knows your situation;
He's always testing your patience,
But His faith is sovereign it's worth waiting;
I am just thankful for whatever wisdom you gave me,
I just pray that it keep saving me.

Blessings

When you were about to fall,
God answers your call;
When you got fired,
But later got hired;
When you are so poor,
Like you can't take it no more;
But then you win the lottery,
Then you're like," what kind of luck I got in me"
Thank God you took another road,
Because the other was a bad episode;
Everything happens for a reason,
All the blessings that keeps pleasing;
Sometimes we get the lesson,
Instead of waiting on the blessing;
So I can't keep stressing,
About this life, can't guess it;
The struggles can come and go,
It's part of life's flow;
Thank God I got blessings, I love them,
Can't really live mistake-free, he blesses and love me still.

Section Four:
RAP

Rap

Welcome to the rhyme that never really ends,
So go ahead, tell a friend;
Care to read this? It all depends,
It is 2010, you going to know I got long wind;

My styles so straight, please don't bend,
I got flows as long as I got a paper and pen;
The rhyme, poet, raps I am like the mixer just blend;

The wisdom I attain you cannot believe;

With God in my life I will only ascend,
If you're not down with that, then you, I must defriend;
God got this thing running so I never have to defend,
And I am always looking to help the needy, this poem my heart
extend;

God is who I recommend,
All His ways I wish I could comprehend;
But that is why I get caught up in sin;
Steady confessing all over again;

I already know I got room to fail,
I cannot be caged in like I am in jail without bail;
I need to have that driving force like wood from a nail;
I want to be delivered by God like United States Priority Mail;

With God in my life I should hold up sturdy like a rail;
My flow's smooth like a boat with a nice sail,
My thoughts overflowed, like water into a pail
My words so serious, expensive thought, forget about a sale;

When I rhyme I am like the reporter, pinpointing detail,

My thoughts are so heavy, try to weigh it on a scale

I am so blessed by God to prevail,
Still got the rhyme, juicy sweet, like ginger ale;

I still rhyme in a positive way, even when times are gray
It is like I am the potter, and my words are the clay;
I get to rhyme yet another day,
I always feel grateful, what can I say?

At that point I just have to pray;
I got the words sweet, like products by Mary Kay;
Have it elegant, sweet like the sunflowers in May;
Knowledge dropped on you so heavy, but you can carry it like hay.

This is real lyric here, no game I am trying to play;
Yet sin will tempt you and eat like you are the prey;

And you know these times are hot like sun's rays,
But you do not have to believe what I say;

I just keep these lines, so I do not go astray,
I wish all the bad vibes just go away;
But it seems we have so much to convey;
And you do not want to go rotten, bad like tooth decay;

How long was this rhyme? Should have been an essay,
But I have to go, put it on display;
But some people hate because I do this so cliché;
But I got so many styles and flavors like Ponderosa's buffet.

Let The Game Take You

I am so down for the game,
Winning is my aim;
If we lose I am to blame,
I am the one with the ball, three seconds left for the fame;

If I fail it is a shame,
In the presses, hard to mention my name;
The momentum was hot like a flame,
And then the end came;

Even with my heavy frame,
I got moves I proclaim;
My skills never the same,
Too much basketball on my brain,

My jumper looking sweet like sugar cane,
Keep others on the court, so twisted up like ankle sprains;
My rhythm so linked up, you'd swear they were chains;
Not tall like cranes, I am posting up, can you hang?

So addicted to the game like I was high off cocaine,
When you talk about free throws, that's when I reign;
Success begins to rub off on me, like a stain,

Because I got basketball seams in my veins;

Doesn't matter the weather, I'm proud to play in the rain
If Damon Wayans showed up, he might say I am a major pain;
I just run on the court like LeBron, a runaway freight train,
They better make me drive, because my shoot they cannot contain;

Even if your moves seem simple, too plain,
That is really all you need to win the game;

My mind is always on the court, sharp like cobra fangs,
Now answer this, do you think you can hang?

So Wrapped in the Rhyme

I stay wrapped in the flow,
Give lyrical blows;
I do these rhymes not just for the dough,
But I got to survive in life you know;

I'm ready for my foes,
Hating my lyrical code;
I am so fly like a crow,
Swoop down I suppose;

I could be sweet like a rose,
Like no one knows;
Go like tortoise slow,
Then sneak attack like the hare goes;

I am so old school, like high waters and Afros
I am way too cold like fans' air mixed with snow;
I might be a lyrical soldier, not your average Joe
Have you like whoa, with the lyrics I throw;

But you probably cannot take that though,
Yo styles probably come up to my toes;
I knew you were not eye level and it shows,
My styles not too far from Edgar Allen Poe's;

I know you thinking like so,
I do not even recognize my glow,
I rhyme like I had shine long ago,
I need to stay humble, hello,
My way just grows;
Intensify more than before,
Forget about too much pride I am like so-so;

Someone might call me a rhyming pro,
But I am just wrapped in the flow;
To nobody but Christ I owe,
My soul because He died for me, yo.

Every Breath Is A Success These Days

See, some people cannot even pray,
Enjoy a beautiful day;
Smell aroma from the river or bay;

We should smile more, stop acting so gray;

We're in life's game, God is the referee over the play;

And in any choice there is always a consequence to pay;
And sin is always trying to eat you like you are prey;

These times are real hot, like the sun's rays,
That is why if I am breathing I still give praise;
I don't care if you do not like what I say,
But I am like Sierra Mist, sweet with these words I spray;

I did this some time ago not yesterday,
And here I am, if still living, blessed today;
You know I got much to confess today;
Every breath is a success today;

GOD Is So Amazing

His mercy blazing,
God is so amazing;
If I am on my knees,
You know who I am praising;

I am a sinner,
But I know my winner;
Even though I got some knowledge,
Compared To Him I am a beginner
Even less than novice oh,
I cannot even hold this you know;
This was laid on my heart
So I put it in flow;

He can have my mind and heart,
Smother my soul;
I have already made many mistakes,
Glad He is so unconditional;

Even if I did not have the mercy
I know where I am going;
See, it is all about God's glory,
His story just growing;

So I live life,
But sometimes I'm wrong,
I cannot do this road alone,
Lord, have mercy, I need You, strong;

Sometimes it is hard to keep it real,
Sin tempts you hard like steel;
You know the ordeal,
Come on, you know how I feel;

But nobody's perfect,
My soul is not worthy;
That's why I always need the amazing God in a hurry.

AMAZING!!

Rapper Or Poet You Make The Call

Some say I am a rapper, some say I am a poet;
I just like to rhyme, most of my friends know it;
I been in this thing about umpteen years,
I just flow like the Mississippi River on paper, keeping things
clear;
Still keep females warm,
Soften them up like hot butter with a poem;
But some think I am a rapper, 'cause I come with cliché metaphors;
but people in the 'hood Know what I am after,
because we all struggle for what we're headed for;
Still low budget chilling,
Rich rhymes are all I am feeling;
Wisdom and knowledge still save me,
Still thankful for what God gave me;
You can call it poetry and you can say it's rhyme,
And you can hate the game but really you're wasting your time;
I just go with the flow,
Let the people know;
How times have really changed
How we are thinking from our own pain;
And then you question whether I am a poet or rapper;
But if you saw me at a concert you would be a clapper.

Rapper or Poet Recall

Am I doing poetry or rapping, you make the call;
But either way you all still clapping; but critics want me to take the fall;
Still say I am cliché with most metaphors,
But I motivate people to open better doors;
But they say I am a rapper, like I got no simile;
But you all know what I am after, I just know they are not feeling me;
I am not a lyricist, but they never let me rock my style awhile to see the real in me;
I can be kosher like pickles, hardcore like things clash;
Soft and sweet like cotton candy, or spice it up hot like Mrs. Dash;
They still question whether I am a rapper or poet,
I got them both twisted like licorice and they should already know

What, You Thought I Could Not Drop It?

See, I bust game,

They can't trust my aim,

Blows with flows that you will understand soon;
My lyrics demand tunes,

Billboard famous like a highway poster;
Put a twist on crowds, does it my way over,

Some will see how I drop it,
They can't knock it;
My lyrics looking like PSP's caught up in a kid pocket
Can't stop it;
I got some so surprised,
Froze like they are hypnotized;
They can't believe their own eyes,
How I drop the lines;
My style can be hard or soft,
Smooth to get some off;

I'm so blended now,
Long-winded now;
My styles can't end it now,
Bad vibes I bend them now;
I just get so critical, some say I'm pitiful;
Rhymes still going a million, just plentiful.

No! Y'all not Ready

These words on point, sharp like machetes;
The flow too strong, until I cannot hold the mic steady;

Have you still untwisting my metaphors? Y'all not ready;

I got the rhyme smooth like harmonious medley,
Keep you so interested true, but really y'all not ready;
Whether it is math or rhyme, I still get some shine;
I only take the recognition, the glory is not mine;
I only write what is real, dropping nothing petty,
You only dealt with the "fake" artist; I told you, y'all not ready.

I Just Know I Got Some Skills

I just spit these rhymes from the heart too real,
I give those lyrical doses like prescriptions that heal;
Give you the right wisdom, feed you like a meal,

You cannot steal my vibe cause I got the patent still;

Words touch your soul because right now you're getting your fill;
I am shocking you like you're the victim and I am the electric eel;
I could be at the bottom of the scope, do not need to be king of the hill,
Because I know I got some skills.

SECTION FIVE:
SUCCESS AND
MOTIVATION

Talk About A Successful Soldier

I flunked the first grade, came back you thought it was all over;
In school was where I stayed, talk about a successful soldier;
Later got honorable mention,
Gave most teachers my undivided attention;
Yet I flew through elementary,
I still did not know teaching was meant for me;
High school came and gone,
I was down for solving the math strong;
I love the challenging situations,
That keep my thought process pacing;
I work for the best,
I love the success;
It's life so you got to contest,
Even with all the stress;
I raced through college,
Tried to attain the best knowledge;
I went through a battle please,
To get my bachelor's and master's degrees;
In math, I look at the world and see numbers;
Some striking like thunder, which makes me wonder;
Failure does not have to be an option;
I'm just a successful soldier and it's non-stopping.

As Motivated As I Got To Be

I steal into life like highway robbery,
being motivated as I got to be;
Don't even care whether I'm rich or poor when people spotting
me;
I'm going to get my kicks, plus I just won't quit;
Me and no motivation are like tape and a bumpy wall, just won't
stick;
But I am not here just mixing metaphors and similes;
I just want to make sure you feeling me,
With this motivation still in me;
You might be reading this lyric, don't just listen, hear it;
It's always telling the truth, you don't have to fear it;
It's like everyday living,
A life God-given;
Long as I am not sinning,
In life I won't be tripping;
Since people like my motivation,
Say it could change a nation;
But I'm still patiently waiting,
On who's participating;
Where is the heart in it, if you don't start in it?
You'll never know unless you take part in it.

But The FLAME Was Still Lit

Just when some thought I was too soft,
Show plays love like golf;
I just need one good birdie by far,
But some women just like me going for pars;
I need to get me an eagle,
A woman that looks so regal;
She's thinking I can't protect her but I'm lethal,
She just doesn't know me in front of people;
Sure I have been through drama,
It's like war with some trauma
But as hard as things get,
If I'm moving, it's because the flame was still lit;
It's like gasoline was poured on my flame,
I get stronger in the game;
Like you mixed my contents with grease,
My flame you envy, so desperate for a piece;
Too hot for you, like a kosher hot pickle;
Maybe comical like laughing hard after being tickled;
My flame kind of tricky, I can be nice or sickly;
I'm just putting lyrics in perspective you get me;
I try to keep my light burning,
Yet I'm still learning.

Clearly Motivated

Clearly motivated,
Like you can't hate it;
You get life how you make it,
If a chance comes you take it;
You only get one physical life, so don't break it,
Life is real as running water, I can't fake it;
And without motivation my thoughts are naked,
I can't get full when I taste it;
Got to have it to do the math,
And to stay on my thinking path;
My soul cleansed like I just had a bath,
Felt free of the wrath;
But I do not have to tell you,
How motivation can sell you;
You think your situation is easy,
Like you're way above failure ;
And you could feel cheap like a penny,
Motivation, I got plenty;

I got to have that straight get up and go;
Can't really just let myself sit up and get old;
Life is what you make it for sure,
Even if you want more;
There is so much in store,
My mind thinking to be rich,
I'm happy though but somewhat poor.

Confidence Calling

It's hard to live life like this,
Always taking risks;
But if everything went perfect
Would living life be worth it?
Feel like a hard puzzle, I'm stuck,
Still afraid of the bad luck;
I need to complete a task, but keep falling
Still though, I hear confidence calling;
I kept my abilities on hold,
Let myself get cold;
So lost in the episode,
Scared to take a certain road;
I'm supposed to have motivation,
But fear blocks my situation;
I want to be comfortable pacing,
No faith is what I'm facing;
My confidence keeps calling too,
I've got to think this through;
Moves looking like hard tasks,
Like there's too much to ask;
I wish some risks were not too bad,
Hope is all we ever had;
Feel like I'm backed to a wall,
Yet confidence just continues to call;
;
I hear it calling in my ear,
Wish my bad thoughts just would disappear;
My confidence keeps calling.

SECTION SIX:
REAL WORLD ISSUES

Pray to God, Only He Knows the Future

The economy keeps slipping, gas prices going crazy at best ,
And strong hard working tax payers are getting hurt with this mess;
And we are not making millions and billions, close to broke, it's chilling;
We thought criminals were only the streets,
But they are on Wall Street too, those villains;

The stock market crashed; times are bad,
All the time I refused to get mad,
With God we can wait on the blessings;
Still persevere in life thru the lessons;
He spared us mercy as we go through these tough times,
I am going to still do my rhymes;

What about that debt you know you cannot pay?
Waking up each and every day with nothing much to say;
Many of us humans are never satisfied anyway;
Some people making billions, too much to share,
But they would rather see poor people suffer, no love there;
That's why the stock market crashed because they don't care.

And why should the poor have to continue to suffer?
I thought America was patriotic, we all supposed to provide a buffer;
So many bad things happen and you wonder if times will be worse,
This is why I will always lean on God first;

We are all just people wanting His Glory,
Everything is all about His Story;
Even with a recession, God can take you through,
If I made it another day, it was His reason for that too;

We are not perfect,

Our lives not worth it;
So many things going on with the human soul;
And God must find ways to let us know, that we really need Him to
grow.

IKE Aftermath,
Galveston, Houston, STL Victim Version

Already bad economical times keep storming,
Then hurricanes and tornadoes come without warning;
You must thank God for being alive to witness,
Even though some may be still sick in ICU,
They need God to handle their business;

Some died with the storm, and you might have lost material
wealth;
But you can replace lost things, but you cannot replace life or your
health;
Times could be worse; you could have lost a loved one too,
And when disasters come we should be caring;
Because we have experiences of going through;

Some people could not rebuild, could not make it to this day;
And I just thank God for giving mercy to evacuees and helping
them on their way;
We'll never know they struggled,
Yet we know they were blessed as they went through trouble;
Disasters could make one go insane, which is why I think about
Christ in my heart and brain.

Gas prices tripping, the nation's economy is chaotic;
I really need faith in Christ and thank God I got it;
My heart goes out to flood victims,
Praise God you make the difference.
Without you in our lives,
What would we do? We could not survive.

The Economy At Christmas Time

I know there is much love to show, especially in this time of year;
And you want to show your appreciation, but the economy's trying
to set you in fear;
You can call me cheap, but really I just want to survive;
You wish some blessings came a little faster, but I am still thankful
that I am alive;

But you still want to show the love
Because your heart feels good when you do;
And you hope sales are really good
For Christmas, because 20 dollars looking more like 2;

You thinking, do you want to buy gifts?
Or save money just for the pump;
Stores really have to lower prices
Just to make the economy jump;

And what about this expensive food?
And what if you need to travel and fly?
You really want to give many gifts,
But Christmas cards seem just fine;

See, we need everlasting faith
Even in our finances still;
Because we can do some foolish spending
Even if it's not in God's will;

I wish times were better
I wish the government could pull this crisis together;
We already take disastrous hits from nature,
But granny always said work with what God gave you.

The economy's looking like enemy number 1,

I got two jobs, still seem hard to get stuff done;
But at Christmas time I look at all the struggles,
There are people going through so much trouble,
And here I am worrying about money,
But God supplied me with breath;
If I am able to get to another Christmas
I am just grateful for that;

It has been a long year
Financially for real;
I am blessed to say Merry Christmas
And it is that time of the year;

Christmas time should never be about financial gifts
But about the Great Spirit that is so uplifting;
When we all work together and get things done
That's exactly how we'll grow and become number 1.

Christmas day is coming, with or without your storm sure enough,
But there has never been a price on showing too much love;
Now you really got to trust God's mercy for your cash now,
Because you are really going to buy gifts whether the economy
picks up or slow down;

But if a millionaire is saving his or her money
How do you think I'm going to feel?
And do not be surprised if you see me
Coming out of the Goodwill;

You might think I am being cheap
Because I wait for every single sale;
But I am just being conservative with my cash
Right here in the STL;

Stores will have to come up with discounts
To make us spend some hard earned money;

We need to feel good about something, why not Christmas?
In order to have faith so we can carry on.

I Must Survive These Economical Times
(The Low Budget Version)

Check it as I drop it
Slow money in my pocket;
You calling me cheap, stop it,
Low budget dollars, don't knock it;

Still fighting through financial storms
That keeps me awake like clock alarms;
The only thing going is these poems
These rhymes keep my heart strong;

Trying to bring it real,
Lyrics you can feel;
We are in some tough economic times still,
You already know the ordeal;

Still broke trying to save money,
Don't care about wants or needs, and to some I gave money;;
Sometimes with loot people behave funny,
While some are well off and still made more money;

Here I want to do better than just survive,
But others just trying to stay alive;
Other countries at each other's heads in war,
And here I am, some worse than me,
Instead there are days, I want more!

Man, times are tough and crazy,
Some people need money and they're not lazy;
We living the **"hard knock life"** right here
Like that song by Jay-Z

I am trying to think like a scholar,

To get them golden dollars;
Hustle or white collar,
I need to survive, believe in God's power;

But if God left me breathing and that's just fine
Free to keep knowledge on my mind;
I've said enough and now it is time, you see I must end this rhyme,
Be blessed my friend and pray to God, to survive these hard times.

How Can One Person Make a Big Change?

You know, divided we fall,
United we grow;
So you know President Obama
Got a place like a hill for sho';

Economy bad, unaffordable healthcare
And opportunities are robbed;
Just thinking about
How so many millions lost jobs;

Thank God I got my two part-time jobs
And my two hustles;
And so much going on
And who said these times had to love you;

Just like we were slow into this mess
It is going to take years to get out;
That is why we all need to vote to put Barack Obama
Back a second term into the White House;

I pray he can give us a change
We can surely believe in;
Economic turmoil or working economy
What you are receiving;

I know some people are mad
But I thought under one nation we grow;
Not just the lobbyists and farmers but
Help out the brother on Section 8 you know;

This was an evolution change
Not just because Barack is black;
A change on the whole nation

As a matter of fact;

See, jobs need to happen
People in Iraq should be at home instead of at bay;
You see how crazy people over there acting
You know they do not want us over anyway;

See, 15 rich billionaires
Will never win a war;
But 350 million working class
People are worth fighting for;

See, we must think smart
So much to fix;
So much has changed as quick
Since the year 2006;

It seems times will be worst
Hot like 100 degrees in a 5-inch thick sweater;
And you think about the consequences,
And they make choices better;

And I am reading this long rhyme
Like a proper man like no other;
But you can the take the brother out of the hood
But not the hood out of the brother;

As a matter of fact,
It is so hard for me to sustain this;
Thinking about the tough times we are in
But I pray Barack can really change it;

Now people are realizing it is time
For all of us to come together;
We need to keep the faith
Like when we step out in rainy cold weather;

And the change will happen in spots
And the gaps will start filling;
And the economy will start to smile,
And everybody got jobs they are feeling;

But this kind of answer takes prayer
And time for real;
And we got to have faith
We can make this happen, not just President Obama still;

And the economy affecting Christmas spirit,
You already know the vision on the seen;
Man, stores was already trying to gift wrap
At Halloween;

Since Gas prices decreasing,
People might get out rent a tree;
Hey I am saving most of my cash
You might call me cheap Hey that is just me;

We all know funds get scarce from
January to that government check;
Even though that next stimulus isn't much
But I wish they tack about four more zeros on that;

I am really hoping for change
All across the globe;
Because you really got people
Dying everywhere you know;

So many foolish reasons,
And some innocent die young;
And I am so blessed I made it to
At least 31;

But change is coming,
And I pray to be here thru it all;
And the struggle rocks may tumble
Some like boulders when they fall;

But really what is comfortable
If you never had it bad;
You never realize you got something
Until it is gone and you miss it and you mad;

And we got someone now
That gives us confidence strong;
And we must have his back,
And have the faith to carry it on;

And I just had to go this flow,
Many rich people foreclosing homes still;
And if you know they are having it bad
Guess who keep money in their pockets for real;

And negative just happen
And I must have faith to walk streets at night alive;
Just like when people just have faith
Whenever they drive;

And the big change is coming,
And I am trying to hold my tears;
And I cannot wait to vote
The next leap year

SECTION SEVEN:
PARTY, R&B, Hip Hop, MOOD

Any Time I step in a Club

Anytime I step in the club,
I need to release some steam;
I just want to run game on a lady
a fine beauty queen;

See, I am the type
Get hype off songs and wall hugging;
Looking for that sweet lady
Eyes on me keep bugging;

You can tell by her winking,
What she kind of thinking;
Something fishy going on
I stared at her, my eyes non-blinking;

I see her waving hi,
While motioning me to come over;
I try to front like I am too shy,
But she creeps up by my shoulders;
I told her whenever I come to clubs,
I got something to release;
It was like a mental war
In my mind and now I got peace;

Seeing all these beautiful ladies
Getting their groove on strong;
I just forget what happened
Last week and what went wrong;

I am just thinking while sipping a drink
That there are more fish in the sea;
And many have been heartbroken
Even you and me;

She said try me on for size,
Can you fill these shoes?
But I hope it is not a surprise,
To set me up for more bad news.

A Different Time

A different time, a different phase,
I still thank God for my days;
I know my soul was not worth it,
Though I must still give Him praise;

So unconditional is God's love,
I must keep praying to hear His mission flow;
I am blessed for my position you know,
I need more of Him to help me grow;

In these tough times,
You could go off in your own mind;
Certain challenges you are not expecting to find
Still got to pray through the grind;

So much has changed,
Everything seems rearranged;
But it does not matter how the blessings came,
The one who allowed them is still the same;

You can go through so much drama,
Put your life on pause like commas;
Halt you like an exclamation,
You are steady praying for your life situations;

Still persevere, still be patient;
Even though having faith is not basic;
But if God allowed you another day,
He spared mercy for you, why not taste it?

It is the joy of another morn,
Grateful if God gave you another day to yawn;
Thank you God from dust to dawn.

I Might Be Too Good for the Radio

Some say my style is too good for the radio,
That is why I publish flows in books but some are still hating
though;
I take it slow, still never to mistake a flow

I just like to rhyme, it is my heart in these living episodes;

Some are scared for the times we are in,
So many tempted to sin;
We know everything looking good is not worth it,
But we were tempted again;

I just rhyme about this, my friend,
So much drama, where to begin?
Struggles I face is like a losing situation,
That's why I am having this conversation

My style is original, fine and genuine,
Words like mines right on time;
But some do not like what's on my mind,
No problem cause everybody may not like my rhymes

Still keep coming tight this time;
I really need to praise God right this time;
Now and forever more
Stay out the dark and His Word every time;
He really will give you a strong solid mind.

I just write a flow then try to top it,
Give me a subject right now I will drop it;
Anything you name it whatever,
But I am not the smartest but I shoot to be clever;

See, I can always get noticed,
I try to rhyme with a focus;
Then brainstorm these ideas,
That comes out magical like hocus pocus;

I come with no top hat or no wand
Just my mind, heart, and soul to bond;
Connecting like molecules
Made from positive and negative ions;

See, I still go through drama by tasting it,
Living life is a choice, cannot waste it;
Certain moves you make get complicated,
Face it some things are not basic;

In these economic times,
Survival just on my mind;
I support people, who support me,
And easy money so hard to find;

But it was really never about the money,
I rhyme because I got this in my soul;
I am so serious like no joking\
Talk about anything I can flow;

Too much for the radio,
So I got more in a book,
Some hate when they see my lines
But others get electric shock shook;

My style you want to try that,
Would you buy that?
Words good for the soul,

Get you hype and ready
That is why I unleash the flow.

Lady You Know You Are Teasing

Lady, you know you are teasing,
Wearing those clothes like you got no reason;
I know I am trying to understand,
You in those clothes trying to get a man;

Looking like you are on a page,
With a title like Beauty of the Year;
And when you are trying to front
I know that is completely clear;

I am walking backwards in my position,
Your beauty in my vision;
And you know I am always searching,
Impressive how your mind's just working;

You know you got it made,
Smile sweet like sugary lemonade;
Already got that modeling style,
Driving a brother wild;

You make it look like mating season,
With the way you are teasing;
Dressed like you are trying to get every man
Pleasure Pleasing;

Beautiful you are,
Sexy style shines like a morning star;
Lady, why don't you put on more clothes?
You are making this so hard;

You looking like a Centerfold's Top Model
Shaped like that glass Coke bottle;
And your swag just too smooth,

So attractive the way you move;

Got me thinking great notions,
You so fresh like the four oceans;
But I already know you can please me,
By the way that you tease me;

You Know Who To Call For The Rhyme

See, my words are right on time,
So you know who to call for the rhyme;
I can drop it fast or ever so slowly,
I got to enjoy life, come on, you're going to know me;

I did the flows for the single ladies,
Those single with babies;
I got rhymes for the married too,
Discrimination, that I cannot do;

Better get each metaphor before you miss it,
I got my styles so twisted;
And If you are trying to get my number,
You will find that I am unlisted ;

I got the rhyme, just throw me a topic,
I am on speed mode just start jotting;
I will keep it real;
And you know no one will top it;

You might even support me with my rhyme
In pocket so drop it;
Don't hate don't knock it;
Some people just like me because I'm creative cannot stop it.

Still got the flow
Some just do not understand;
When I die I hope I got a math book
Or a pen and paper in hand;

See, it is not about the millions,
It's about God giving me this talent to rhyme;
I would rather be broke for God,

Than rich for sin at any given time;

All this is in my soul
Still down for success you know;
I only got one fleshly life to live,
So you know whom to call to rhyme,
You know in your soul how much love for it I give.

I Am Just Being Me

It was never about my story,
It was all about His Glory;
My ways cannot be trusted,
Just last week my eyes lusted;

I hate that word called SIN,
Sometimes even tempted to give in;
But I need to hold resistance longer,
God please make me stronger;

I am just being me, I guess,
So human just like all the rest;
I already know my soul's not worthy,
And if you reading these lines I know that you heard me;

God I pray to keep me in line,
I get so distracted at times;
I know I have been oh so wrong,
But I got victory with believing in You life long;

See, any day my lifestyle could tumble,
This is why I stay humble;
And I believe in God and I cannot wait
Until He calls my number;

But until then I am caring,
I give now, I am sharing;
Break off a little of my soul,
I hate to be too proud,
I don't want to forget,
the One who blessed me so;

I need to pray for faith longer,

Persevere it, no hurry;
I need to love people better
Like God spared me mercy;

See, I am just being me
God had allowed us all to live at this time;
And I will never forget about God
Whether I am loose or caught in a grind.

Fall In It

You listening to my song, you all in it;
You grooving too strong, about to fall in it;
Got nice clothes on, like you balling a minute
Don't stop my song, let's stall a minute;
Got to play my lyrics, in this hall a minute;
People move when they hear it, they all in it;
Got the song for a summer, let's halt a minute;
Let's take it low under, get off in it;
Club mixes, I can do that, rock the show;
Fall up in it true that, cop the flow;
Long as I got you to move, it was not hard for sho';
You more than loose, got you doing more;
What you thought I could not drop it? I'm Mister Hyper;
You're falling in it, can't knock it, the lyric tighter;
Got some dancing crazy, having a ball with it;
I just need to grab a lady, and just fall in it.
You know I got to hold it down now,
I got the lyrical game and gone now;
On the floor I got to clown now,
It's going to be on now.

At a Mic

At a mic,
I can sooth your soul;
Emotions like, loose not cold;
With my tools like carpenters, I know what I'm after,
You feel it like an interesting sequel my lyrics shackled your
capture;
At a mic,
Create a visual picture,
Like, it's real how it hit you;
I'm not even psychic,
But hypnotic minds won't like it;
At a mic,
I can,
Mess with your rhythm in plans,
You like putty in my hands;
Feed into my demands;
At a mic,
I can spit the parable,
The wisdom never terrible;
It's looking so like us,
It's human's style, type us;
At a mic,
I could control the flow;
Get it hype, to levels I can't know;
At a mic,
Keep some interested and warned,
It struck them like the severity of a storm;
At a mic,
I blast,
Like I was an outcast;
Still spit slow like I'm placing last,
Just so I don't show up too fast....
At a mic.

Talk About A Successful Soldier

I flunked the first grade, came back you thought it was all over;
In school was where I stayed, talk about a successful soldier;
Later got honorable mention,
Gave most teachers my undivided attention;
Yet I flew through elementary,
I still did not know teaching was meant for me;
High school came and gone,
I was down for solving the math strong;
I love the challenging situations,
That keep my thought process pacing;
I work for the best,
I love the success;
It's life so you got to contest,
Even with all the stress;
I raced through college,
Tried to attain the best of knowledge;
I went through a battle please,
To get my bachelor's and master's degrees;
Yes, in math, look at the world I see numbers;
Some striking like thunder, some gone under;
Failure does not have to be an option;
I'm just a successful soldier and it's non-stopping.

Beat the Floor Down

It is about to go down,
Beat the floor down;
Now you know now,
You got moves to show now;
Your dance moves come correct,
Others get no respect;
They just move their body what the heck,
Some just flex pop their neck;
Slide to the left,
Then to the right;
It does not matter if their moves not tight;
Pump dance to robot,
It does not matter; give just what you got;
I am just here to have fun,
If you are worried about weight I am one-tenth a ton;
I just want to move on it,
Groove on it;
I am coming with the rhyme so smooth on it;
Like you want my vibe, yeah you want it;
Got you loaded,
My style you want to hold it;
You cannot bite because I got it coated;
I just got to move to stay in shape,
I wear clothes big like I am in a cape;
Like I am trying to be a hero,
On the floor;
I do not save souls, I just peep dances more;
Plus I must clown,
See who beating the floor down.

Can I Get You To Do This?

Can I take you to your legs? Can I get you to your feet?
Can I get you to move yeah, rock your body?
Can I get you to dance?
Move more in your pants?
Give a brother a chance;
I'm already in my stance;
Now bounce tells the world that holds it down (us);
You know we like to clown;
Can I get a holler from the crowd? (Yell)
State your presence really loud
Boom, we like Q-tip song just vibrant things;
Get our biz let it all hang;
Still got you into this song I sang;
And still the crowd runs the game;
Can I get you to do it just like this?
Egyptian twist moves in your wrist;
Got you to move you mobile right now;
I want the whole world to see like it's global tight now;
My skills complete, almost like total right now;
This is so hot like women in a see through overnight gown;
Got you to jam, you can't ignore my hype now;
I am letting it go on the mic right now;

Choreo Poem

Now windmill your right arm around,
Then do the left and touch the ground;
Go ahead get frog with your knees,
You doing this for you so do not get fancy with me;
Raise up now, bend back,
Then go to the front relax;
Now right foot step,
Then left foot step;
Twist your hip to the right,
Get that abdomen tight;
Then to the left, just roll your neck;
Hands out, just stretch,
Tighten up like you trying to flex;
Now down on your knees,
Make an angle with your legs forty-five degrees;
Then throw your back way back,
Flex just like that;
Take one leg out to the front,
Keep the other bent, go how low you want;
I am just here to sweat,
And get you to choreograph this yeah;
Perspire let's go,
This flow hot you know;
Stand up kick your leg one time,
Like you the cheerleader kind;
Get loose like you are crunk;
You do not want to be like trash, so let's move that junk.

This Is The Lyric You Dance To

I got the right words to your body
If you got body to the music;
Keep up with the pace player
Yes don't lose it;

With all that shaking and baking
I am interested in what you making;
Your dance moves so ill,
Just no faking;

Rhythm so fast might
Have your body aching,
If your moves on point
You will be up for the taking;

Got it hot like a heater,
You cooler than a fan;
You just a dancing machine to my
Lyrical intent, you understand;

My lyrics like your gas,
And you like the car;
When both these come together
There is a shine like a shooting star;

I go for what I know,
You got the beat down in this flow;
From here your style can only grow,
You feel the vibe in your nerves no;

And you can only beat yourself,
Forget about competitive help;
You are the dance champion among nations,

Where is your style I am still waiting?

You know I got the lyric smooth
So bring on them dance moves;
So I can fall into your groove,
Show the world you got nothing else to prove.

Section Eight:
TOPIC POETRY

Hope Must Be On The Way

So many layoffs,
It is no payoff;
Job security looking so lost,
I just think about an employee as an opportunity cost;

Now the faith rocks must tumble,
Your job might be on the line;
You cannot really talk about recession-proof
When things get worst in time;

So many food born illnesses
So many things to think about too;
And the faith of the economy looking lost
You looking like what is next to do;

You might have to invent something
Millions in this world can use;
I am just glad if I got two jobs,
Blessed I had not been hit with some bad news;

See, mercy held me today
If I am still alive;
There must be hope of a better day,
Because people scared to take risks just survive;

And who wants to buy a house,
If your job security is on the brink;
See, this economy can play with your emotions,
Until you really can barely even think;

And who wants to take that risk,
You want to be so ahead of the game;
You build on all this debt,

And it can drive you insane;

But at least I can still breathe,
Some are living worst;
And I have no health insurance,
But I just think about God first;

And so many bad things could happen
Glad it is not terribly chaotic for real;
But God woke me up another sunny morning,
And put me on my way, so hard like steel;

See, if I made it another moment,
It was not for my glory;
I might be blessed on it,
But it was a big part of His story;

See, I never know why things happen
Why things go the way they do;
But I know if I am still alive,
It was His reason for that too;

But the hope of change is coming,
Something we all can believe in for real;
It is such a shame when a bad economy
Just change your career options still;

Now you got people seeking recession-proof,
But really is that true;
Job security has no foundation,
And what if the company
gets bought or go into bankruptcy too;

I am figuring out the nation more,
As I get older and such;
But a fifty-year old man in 2009

Will still say I am a young buck;

So many changes has happened,
So many more changes on the way;
Never thought the government
Would ever have to give us an economic jump to be okay;

And it is already so violent,
And so many kids are always born;
And with a diving economy
So many things really cannot get done;

And more monopolies might happen,
Because consumers go to who they choose;
I am so grateful to God
If I am still breathing to live for Him too;

Hope must be on the way
Because it gets worst before it gets better;
So many things wrong
And times hot like 3-inch wool sweater;

But thru all the drama,
If I am alive, God spared the mercy,
Now I know more why it is privilege to survive
I know somebody heard;

The hope of a better tomorrow
Where the economy gets back strong;
People got the jobs they want,
And entrepreneurs can hustle and carry on;

And hopefully times will be like a flower's bloom,
And many people will be able to provide for their space and room;
And sometimes you feel mercy is really all you have left,
See, someone been sick with congestion can understand my breath;

And some people going thru worst,
So why should I even plead;
When I have been after so many wants
And not what I really need;

But we want the hope of a better tomorrow,
When sometimes we are not really in line;
That is why I thank God for any moment
Because we could be in the worst of times.

Black History

Black History
These are the ancestors of choice;
And when things were not right
They lifted up their voice;

They sacrificed in times of struggle
Took the bill in the hustle;
Made a dream for the country to wonder
Moves these people made struck like thunder;

More opportunity was open,
The chains on minorities broken;
No more limits or pressure,
From King to Obama, now we go get the measure;

Black History I still treasure,
Ancestry held out in pain;
Just to make more opportunities
For minorities to do more things;

See, we cannot blame,
Our people struggled thru some times;
And I was not even alive when they were
But I can vibe it in this rhyme;

Black History
Allowed opportunity to make it thru college,
That was the reason
I got good wisdom and knowledge;

And Black History was the motivation
To be a great person for the nation;
And change was already done in a sense,

President Obama, hey that's no coincidence;

See, Black History made an embryo,
And now we get to see it bloom;
It used to be in a tight spot,
But now it has hot balloon air room;

So much opportunity now to witness,
So get yo education and handle your business;
Keep faith in one hand, hope in the other
We must continue the shine
of our past courageous sisters and brothers

Black History paved the way for the Hope
Of a better tomorrow;
Even with all the struggles
And past sorrows;

The members of Black History
Laid the confidence more like a foundation strong;
See, when I think about their sacrifices,
It pumps me to be successful lifelong;

See, you thought it would never happen,
But now we asking about how many more;
I am talking about the Presidency
And a thousand other things minorities can now explore;

And we got the critical minds
Because we have been thru critical times;
See, some know what it means to be poor,
So low until you cannot take it any more;

But if God left me still breathing,
I must pass the Black History torch;
I must be blessed for any moment

Because these times are hot like a sun's scorch;

So many times have changed,
Yet, so many things stayed the same;
It seems you already carry a strike,
Before you even introduce your name;

But Black History is the reinforcement,
That keeps us going strong;
It might be assumed that we will fail
But we will struggle for success with the game and gone;

See, when a minority makes a mark,
It will never be forgotten;
And times could be hard and tough,
or smooth and gentle soft like cotton;

Black History leaves rights open in spots,
Success is on the rise we must always keep that hot;
Yeah this heritage yes this is for me,
I am so grateful for our month in BLACK HISTORY;

Pride or No Pride

When I was young I used to be conceited,
Knowledgeable about my subjects like I knew I succeeded;
But then, the most humble felt better and opened up their heart,
I was a hothead like I could even start;
Never really realizing why math was in my picture,
I never knew in six years after college
how hard teaching math could get you;
Before, I had too much pride,
did not want to share anything with others;
Even wanted to show up my sisters and brothers;
And the motivation and determination was really not mine,
It was God's faith that allowed me to get in line;
But He has the shine and all the praise,
Because some have had worst days;
I am so humble now it's a shame,
If I could I would share my name.

Nervous

It's the pen shaking,
The weird drawings you making;
The shaking at the altar,
When you feel you going to falter;
It's the bad answers at the interview,
That you pretended to;
Praise so strong,
But you came in the wrong;
like you actually knew the words,
But in front of people the recite is unheard;
You get that strange twisting tongue,
And then you stutter so long;
Then people count your um's,
Like it's some ghetto song;
Then, it's times you are nervous when you think it is gone;
You know you are falling apart but you still struggle on;
It's that feeling inside,
That comes out when the adrenaline rise;
But you will know most times it's no sneaky surprise;
Teeth shaking like you scared, but just a little nervous there;
Like it's the hardest obstacle that you ever dared;
Others may see your struggle, know the trouble;
It already popped like a bubble.

Guilty?

Your mind is like a question mark,
Where you got to guess to start;
Your hormones like a snake,
In the moves you make;
Like you are wearing two left shoes,
Before taking the step to get bruised;
Thoughts so passive, took long to come;
But there exist this situation but you still run;
It's like you walking on thorns,
Holy shoes on;
So confused, still like it was sunny,
During a thunderstorm;
Like a fever, feel warm but you cold,
Your body won't let you know;
You try to protect your cover,
Your guilty conscience makes you smother;
The guilt suffocates your mind,
You start thinking crooked at times;
Just barely getting through each day,
Whether or not you pray;
You still recognize your guilty ways,
Like a sad, nasty filth taste;
But the truth hurts,
Holding guilt in sometimes don't work.

Danger!

Everything so black,
So vulnerable in any type of attack;
Everything keep falling apart,
Nothing nice ever starts
LOVE only matters when something bad is at heart;
And you want to be alarmed,
your adrenaline is warned;
But you get bitten, then your realization is all torn;
All the good is gone,
Some bad song playing on;
At this point you can't be strong;
Cause a consequence has won;
Your thoughts be too late,
Can't watch the moves you make;
It happened so that you don't realize the mistake;
Its color is blood red,
But the daring never stopped instead,
People never realized until the blood is on their head,
Or they are dead!
But this is so serious,
Then people curious;
How people don't blush
They run into trouble on the rush;
They get burnt like bacon; crisp like cereal flaking;
Its danger in the making.

Desperation

It's like a beast after me
Who has devoured prey and is still hungry;
It's not chaotic or wild actually
It's already got what it wants, see;
It's like a risky gamble
It infected your mind, you out of control;
Your adrenaline race you scramble
Blocking the thought to your soul;
It got you like a time bomb
You ready to go off at any second;
You don't want it to come
Your emotions run wild you sweating;
It makes you blame your intentions
When you truly made the move;
This is not a new invention
It's a consequence in all things people do;
You in too deep feel like a furnace
Like there is no turning back;
You understand the lesson you learning
But you persistent in learning that.

Section Nine:
SURVIVAL RHYMES

Prayer And Hope Is All You Got

I can see the joy in another morning,
But that pink slip comes without warning;
This air you still breathe and taste it,
The hope of the best life you must hold out
until heaven just to face it;

You keep on seeing violence,
Like people was raised in silence;
See, what happened to moral right and wrong,
So much been accepted yeah, the old way is gone;

You wonder why health problems arise,
See, some people cannot eat like that affluent gal or guy;
Some people was just born into a situation,
Some people had to work hard in their occupation;

Work hard for little knowledge,
That little bit made me author, years after college;
Always been a poet still my life a race,
God owns the stopwatch and grateful if He spared grace;

So much bad could happen awhile,
But I am like service with a smile;
I figure if I always kept a frown,
Nothing positive would go down;

Still go through much drama,
But yet God allowed me breath;
See, even if I had no job,
Grateful if I got my limbs good health;

These economic times are a struggle,
But we have to muscle through this okay;

And sometimes all you got left is the Hope
And you just have to pray;

See, I figure it must be a reason if I am
Still alive at this point in time;
Because everybody's number will be called
I surely have mine.

Just a Survival Writer

I am just a survival writer, what else can I say;
I go through twist and turns just to get past a day;
And sometimes I cannot do nothing but push boulders slowly
That is how heavy some struggles get before me;
Still thank God if I can breathe,
I need his faith before I roll up my sleeve;
Some who struggles in life
hate to have to taste it;
Sometimes you wish life was like some math so basic,
let us face it;
You just wishing you were wisdom gifted,
But you need some prayer just to get uplifted;
You pause just to reminisce the blessings,
Since you know others going through worst lessons;
And now you see why I am blessed if I am alive,
Still writing, thank God if I survive.

Survive

You can hate me,
Try to break me;
Attempt slow my road,
But I got to pick up and go;
If I'm breathing its for a service,
I can't be nervous;
I can't be like that lion on the
Wiz of Oz I got to have courage;
I got to fight through the Hard-Man Struggle;
I got to be a survivor like Destiny's Child say because
Some of the world hate to love you;
I got ghetto tendencies as a means to survive;
So cheap I skip items that cost ten somewhere else it's five;
This is how I stay alive, save money;
Even if I had good-to-go dough, I gave money;
I still got to give,
Right now low budget is how I live;
Thank God I'm here every second,
It's just an opportunity so he let it;
Living life is like getting close to the sun so I sweat it;
I got to survive while I live I can't forget it;
I still got to eat,
Move to the store, sore in my feet;
I got to take a bus, can't afford to finance a car right now and such,
Survival looking tough.

Thank God If I'm Still Alive

I have had painful abscesses,
Bowel movements that gave me stress;
Don't eat healthy like most of the rest,
But If I'm still alive I am surely blessed;
My blood pressure was deadly high,
Like I could barely get by;
My fatigue played out,
Like I was really on my way out;
But I was able to type this poem,
To share the story so pass this on;
I got my issues yes,
Plus I try to do my best;
Then again I still go through drama,
Having all the weight put my life on pause like commas,
I got so many who cares for my life but why,
I only chose to live for God;
This life is not the final resting place,
Look at all these crazy diseases we have made ourselves to face;
God did not say eat that nasty grease taste,
The fruit is always good to eat into waste;
But I'm surprised I'm still alive,
So much on this planet bad you can get poisoned and die;
I'm just blessed if I can still survive...

Walking Through The Storm

I cannot deny it,
It's my life I got to try it;
Every step looking like a hustle,
Still got to move my muscles;
Feels like I am fighting through tough rocks,
Two hands all I got;
I got to race through the flame,
The heat is all too strange;
I must give my all,
So many depending on me not to fall;
I cannot give in,
If I quit, my life cannot begin;
See it takes motivation,
To get through some situations;
Faith in God is what I am faced with,
Yet struggles seem basic;
But I got to be patient, let us face it;
I cannot be perfect so why chase it,
But we still must work to survive,
Stay alive;
I know we cannot live above the norm,
But we got to walk through the storm;
The grips may take hold,
But I must have the faith to get through episodes;
The walk looking hard, but I must be smart;
I cannot break apart,
I should be able to do it,
But God knew it.

I'm Gon Still Rise

I' m gon' still rise,
The vision in my eyes;
The whole world hypnotized,
They surprised;
How I made it,
They can't fade it
God had it that way,
It was anticipated;
I'm still human,
My styles be zooming
I still hustle and hang,
Straight do my thing;
With the help of God things happen;
Whether I make it in education or make it rapping;
And my mom couldn't help me, dad left me at 2 weeks old;
I'm off to live life,
to find out things I need to know;
My granny kept me living strong,
Was my backbone;
Gave me the advice to get on;
I still got to kick it,
But can't live too wicked,
your life is how u pick it.

Section Ten:
TOTALLY METAPHORICAL

Bad

The darkness unfolds,
Like an evil episode;
The vision sightless,
Where you don't like it;
Like a filthy needle poking,
Or gagging while choking;
Taken like your last breath,
Haven't got an ounce left;
Wicked iniquities and filth,
Spoil you dry like milk;
You get so blind,
And forgetfulness enters your mind;
You cut into danger,
And neglect the helpful stranger;
And yet still wicked, your veins will only respond to anger;
On the road you gamble and lose,
And try to punish the abused;
Then you wonder why the unwanted joke is on you;
You never blush,
Mind so violent in the rush;
Then you wonder why you can't be with a spouse you can trust;
Like you got no lights, no air, its no fair;
No water for thirst, no food hungry in the worst
Like a head on collision,
Interrupting your life mission;
Lethal in your present position,
Cut you like an autopsy incision.

Captured

I'm so locked down,
Like I'm shackled now;
Like I'm caught in someone's arms,
Not free like most poems;
My emotions so immobile,
Feel like my life is over;
Like all I saw was the net,
The gross I'll never get;
You feel so caught up,
Mind all thought up;
Like you ran out of schemes,
Lost all self-esteem;
To get loose I tried my best,
Felt like I was never close to success;
It's looking like my final chapter,
I feel so captured;
Like nothing would work,
I tried much erk and jerk;
Like ants trapped in a can,
Moving without a plan
Like someone put your life on pause,
This vision is all you saw;
You keep thinking things will change,
For a while everything is the same;
Thank God I'm still alive,
My purpose is to survive;
Living life stuck in a world of desperate rage,
I might as well be in a cage;
So captured yes,
But I still got this air in my chest 'til the day I rest.

Meta - Flow - ric

I'm like a hot headline,
In the New York Times;
Lyrics be fine,
Like two-spaced writing on lines;
Better keep up with the times,
Because I will leave you behind;
I am still low budget I am not lying,
Still tossing dimes;
Lyrics can be soft like melted butter,
Close hard like shutters;
Flow be like water through gutters,
So nice the world stutters;
Just a meta-FLOW-ric strong,
I can't go wrong;
Metaphors and flows quick and long;
Like communications with phones;
I did this on my own,
Note the tone;
In this unique poem,
Sing it like a song;
The power is in the words,
If you haven't heard;
Mind sharp like a nerd,
Me not writing that's absurd;
I got to write out my problems, like math work on paper;
My mind and attitude work with my behavior;
I'm like a journalist,
got to write it down,
I got pages now;
I will be seen for ages now...

Some Label Me A Rap Artist

Some label me a rap artist,
But they do not want to start this;
I am more like a tricky poet,
Ask my friends in Saint Louis
yes they know it;
Still keep lyrics running hot like a toaster,
Still legit in the rhyme
trying to do what I am supposed to;
Got so many styles
just call me the chameleon of lyrics,
Be around another style
just shift accordingly so you can hear it;
Yet still looking original and smooth with my style
I cannot lose it,
And do not hate my style
just because you cannot abuse it;
I could write just in metaphors,
You see what I am heading for;
I am not looking to settle scores,
I am looking to open better doors;
But they label me a rapper instead of a lyrical poet,
I am always well personified
and critics should know it.

The Metaphoric Man

I am sweet like sugar,
Could be nasty like a bugar
cold like ice,
Act white like rice;
Can get hot like heater,
Adventurous like Pan comma Peter;
Still cool like a fan,
I am like the thought you don't understand;
I am like rhythm in the rhyme,
Flow be on time;
I am like icing on the cake,
Sealing up moves that I make;
I am like the nail in the coffin, close out the show for good;
I am the ghetto vibes on your street, people know I'm all hood;
I am that critical being on the street,
Got you by two feet;
That's the way I think,
So that my plans don't stink;
I'm the new rhyme man on the block brothers are you ready for it;
I am going to keep going I'm the man that is metaphoric.

Section Eleven:
STRAIGHT LYRICAL

Straight Lyrical

See, somebody told me I could rhyme
This style I just flow it;
Never knew I could write stories, raps,
Songs, rhymes and still be a poet;

Straight lyrical when I drop it,
On any topic;
I like to keep some in my pocket,
Don't hate don't knock it;

I figure it was about that time,
To introduce my book of rhymes;
Try to fuel the economic grind,
So much going on in my mind;

So I got this creation,
To put a shock on the nation;
All this came from the heart I had to start this
And people wonder how can he
be a math teacher and spoken word artist;

See, I just take real life situations
Charge it to a rhyme;
You already know these times we are facing,
Be thankful if you got a job on the grind;

See, I got similes and metaphors,
Lyrical shots you ready for;
Present the rhyme clever,
My alias name is SLYK so you should know me better;

Have the ladies in awe,
But these words they heard or saw;

Sweet and soft like candy cotton,
With the way I drop it how can I be forgotten;

God always blesses me well,
Granted me to think of flows;
But I am so grateful I have a pen
So let them go.

My Lyric Needs No Introduction

My lyric needs no introduction,
Haters get sucked in;
It's my styles they be loving,
Wear it like hand-gloving;
And I do not have to tell you,
How my lyric can sell you;
I'm motivated in success,
Just no failure;
So open your eyes,
'While I jump out my scary disguise;
And bring the heat like I make others realize;
I let the pen to the paper,
It works with my behavior;
When dealing with problems
writing them out sometimes save you
My lyrics be serious,
Readers be curious;
People already living my lyric,
They still hearing this;
They know the going vibe,
The change in some people's lives;
How nowadays it's hard just to survive;
I write lyric that is real,
The most words people feel;
I come down hard like steel,
When describing ordeals;
Still it seem so genius,
The lyric how I mean it;
Even if it looks dirty it's
The truth so I can't clean it.

It Is No Surprise

It is no surprise how I drop it,
On any topic;
Haters be like stop it,
Do it up at the cockpit;
To the lady I just poem,
Their feelings storm;
I have no pride strong,
it is just a lyrical song;
Keep it clever-minded,
Like a secret cannot find it;
And you glued to my style get a listen in
your mind and rewind it;
I just write what is on my mind,
The truth so hard to find;
I said the flow would be on time,
All caught up in rhyme;
It is no surprise how I do this,
Myspace friends already knew this;
Leave some clueless,
Others think SLYK SLYVEE who is this;
or who is that,
With the lyrics too phat,
so blowed up like cells too tapped;
I come with no disguise,
Just lyric before your eyes;
Totally it is no surprise,
How I drop these lines.

LYRICAL Access Granted (2007)

Come on let us get with it,
You know I had to spit it;
When I rhyme I cannot lose it,
It is a skill cannot abuse it;
Just had to keep you informed,
Whether rap or poem;
I know some cannot stand it,
I got the lyrical access just granted;
See now I got some to move,
Never realized how my lyric do;
I just had to bring it still,
Sometimes it is words you can feel;
It might ease your mind,
Keep you in a grind;
Some good lyric hard to find
You hear mine then rewind;
I got to keep it grooving,
Keep the flow moving;
If you start to feeling me,
It is because you got the simile;
Then I toss in metaphors,
To show you what I am heading for;
It is all in my lyric,
Got you locked in when you hear it;
I write it because I love it,
Only God above it;
So much going on this nation,
I can write about every situation;
I do not care about a rhythm,
It's nice lyric I give it.

Lyrical Battle in a Ring

You going to know how I run this,
Lyrics drop like mad guns that hits;
My flow-spirit storm,
Yours not even lukewarm;
I lyrical battle do my thing,
Like boxers swing in rings;
Drop combos at the mic,
When you not the rapping type;
I let off heat people sweating, you misting;
You scared kitty kat running while I'm big fisted;
It's important you get every metaphor before you miss it,
You not ready for how I just ripped it;
You need to pivot,
That wack lyrical you give it;
Hope when you rhyme that's not the lifestyle you living;
Poor,
Battling you I can't take it more;
What am I wasting my time for,
There's more to explore;
I battle fight through the mic,
Jabs how I like;
I toss knock out rhymes,
People passed out before I finish one line;
I have brought the fire, maybe I should retire;
Maybe give another a chance to bring down to the wire.

Lyrical War 2004

I'm coming like storms,
Hail be the norm;
If you battle me it's like a tornado warn;
If you battle me I make your speech foreign;
Lyrically I'm a hero like Spiderman mixed with spawn;
You like a pawn, I'm like the queen;
Giving you ferocious rapping that enemies never seen;
Leave you with no esteem, ready to join my team;
It will look like I blasted you with a super beam;
So you know what I mean I'm settling the score;
I'm just not wasting time mixing similes and metaphors;
It's a lyrical war its not going to be a treaty;
Just the best flow ammunition really won't beat me;
I'm a keep going until I get five mics;
I'm rapping non-stopping, yeah alright;
So come on people get at me if you want more;
It's going down Lyrical War 2004;

Section Twelve:
HOLIDAY and BIRTHDAYS

What You Thought I Could Not Rhyme About Christmas Time

What you thought I could not rhyme,
Even at Christmas time;
Come on now we almost through another chapter;
Jesus Christ birthday is happening;
You better give thanks and honor you're even alive,
You know many did not make it,
And Mercy and Grace is golden so you got be blessed and take it;
And you should be thankful if you was able to read this rhyme,
Some probably came from Iraq really blind;
See, its so much to take into account in your position landed,
Some people still broke but breathing still can stand it,
while others are stuck stranded;
Did not even care about getting a gift,
I just had faith that Christ would give me a greater lift;
Make me realize and understand,
This life is never about me in this land;
It's about nature of the world,
And this goes out to every man, woman, boy and girl,
Have a spirit-filled Christmas.

This Not Just Another Christmas Rhyme (2007)

This is not just another Christmas rhyme,
Well we all should spread joy and love not just at Christmas time;
Experience the gift of giving,
This is the life we should be living;
Helping out each other one by one;
It should be peace and harmony beautiful like the morning rising sun;
We must understdid not make to this day,
Just for that we should have a big Kool-Aid smile on our face;
And when the nice flakes float and all ,
We need to flourish peace and love everyday even in the Spring, Summer, and Fall;
So pick up your head and be grateful for God's mercy and cheer,
And just be thankful if you made it because Christmas is near.

Talk About A Birthday

We can talk about another birthday
Because some do not last another moment in time;
I thought I said I would be serious it is worth it
That is why I had to go this rhyme;
And the engine is blessed to keep going
And the gas is the wisdom one find;
And with birthdays there is experience
Which help with the faith and the knowledge of the mind;
So I told you this goes deep like the Grand Canyon strong;
Be proud to celebrate your birthday,
Because you never know how many more must go on;
after your birthday you are wiser, and changes you began to feel;
What you began to know came to surprise ya,
and your faith got closer to steel.

Happy Thanksgiving

Happy give thanks it is a time of sharing and cheer;
Give Christ praise that I am still here;
So much going on, you cannot stop the presses;
So many crazy times, so many learning lessons;
Sometimes it is hard to absorb life's essence;
But we experience so many blessings;
And with our families we keep in touch;
We need to have that communication because times are tough;
And so much grace got us coming along,
We must have faith and be strong even now;
It does not matter rich or poor we all face tribulations and trials;
So much be going on,
This is why we must give thanks strong;
And the love is in the air you know,
It is just nice to have a gracious soul;
In your life you feel better yes,
When you open up your heart at your best.

HAPPY THANKSGIVING!

Everybody Has A Father

Everybody has a Father, at least all who believe;
And He spared mercy and I am grateful if that is all I should
receive;
See, we could do the worst, yet God loves us still;
I thought I said this would get deep, that is a true Father for real;
And He got your helpful answer, but it is on His time,
And I am just a twig and He started that root the whole nine;
And you have a Father,
Already knows your living design;
And I have no knowledge of my future, I cannot even see the
signs;
But my Father loves me no matter what I do or say,
And what kind of human will love you that way.
Now that is a father!

Section Thirteen:
THESE TIMES

Be Satisfied

I am still breathing, thank God,
I got through some unbeatable odds;
Just pushing with my guard,
I know life is hard;
I know when your body is not straight,
Hate making mistakes;
Still satisfied,
I realized some yesterday died;
I got to still live life enough to taste it,
It is looking quite basic;
But it's not an easy road let's just face it,
Can't waste it;
These words of wisdom, motivate my position;
I know some wishing
They had my vision,
But your life was planned to go through troubles,
Some tough struggles;
In any event God will always love you,
He's above you;
And if you around another day,
That's a blessing in itself to pray,
Don't take for granted what I say;
This is not a sermon, I am no preacher;
You probably read it before; I'm a math schoolteacher;
I got nothing to hide,
I should be so satisfied.

Thankful For The Rough Times, May 2008

I just thank God for the rough times, because incidents could be
much worst;
Man we could have no power for months, and then we are dying of
thirst;
See, we could have enough, and still not satisfied;
and some people living in poverty with out a door
At least we can get in out the rain when it comes by;
Some just so homeless, And then I am worried about the loans I
cannot pay;
And then economy might be messed up no doubt, but at least I
am alive to witness it okay; See, I had to bring this from my soul
Because this all the vision that I see;
See, I know I had some wrongs, yet God still had mercy on me.

Facing Hard Times (May 2008)

I just caught a cold, sinus just tripping;
So costly now times is slipping;
What is with the change?
so hard to make cash,
Thankful if I do not go hungry
because I do not know if I could last;
These times are real no joking;
Now I see why many people stressed out smoking;
what is with this route?
Hard to even get a good house
Life looking like a dead rose,
Just starving for rain,
Blessed if I can still survive I suppose;
While some others mentality insane;
Even with these hard times, education is the answer;
But some of your communities looking so diseased like cancer;
How can business function,
When you got all this dysfunction;
It is not their fault they facing hard times,
And that is why I hold my guard in these lines.

Fight Thorns and Boulders, May 2008

At first I was fighting thorns in my life they are like simple cuts
and bruises;
But struggles are like them boulders like it is an arm or a leg I am
losing;
and emotions are not physical, the pain on the inside slowly goes
away;
They were not like those thorns
Those simple bruise that healed okay;
See, some boulders are like tattoos that cannot be moved;
And some struggles are lessons that bring out the better in you;
And some struggles you want to run from
Because your faith is not stronger;
And I wish I knew the right answer
I guess I must pray a little longer;
Why was I crying about thorns?
When I need to make sure the boulders are gone

Roll With the Pushes 2008

You just roll with the pushes,
Like you fighting through sticky bushes;
But you are a fighter, yes
You refuse to get stressed;
It must be a purpose smooth,
You cannot be nervous in what you do;
And the heavy wind will try to hold you,
But you roll with the pushes like a soldier;
And the stripes is spiritual faith,
You sometimes get no reward,
Why do you think God gets the glory while you explore?
He wants to see us shine,
But the mentality may not be mine,
And why should you take the credit,
You should know it was God embedded;
And He will take you through some storms,
You will be thanking Him if you see another morn.
Be blessed.

Section Fourteen:
SOFT POEMS

These Ladies Got Me Softer

These ladies got me going soft,
That is why I beautify the flow;
But what other way is there
To impress a lady by the sweet love you show;

See, the softer I am
The better off she feel;
See, I must change my mood this way
In order to be fine with nice women still;

They got me saying poems of love
When I am trying to go for peace;
And I do not know we cannot figure it out
What is happening on our city streets?

See, that is why I write about mercy,
Because that is a golden word having faith you have some fear;
See, I know someone heard me,
But thru it all I am just thankful for standing right here.

Still the ladies got me being softer,
Talking about poems of love;
Not the filthy sort of lust
But the caring part sure enough.

A Lonely Heart

Sometimes my heart gets so lonely,
Section off from me;
Feel like so much pity on me,
Got me so decrepit, my nerves break,
Got to watch the moves I make;
Don't want to be weary in my way,
Since I'm lonely in the play;
I am like a card stack breaking down,
Someone take me now;
What have I done?
Feel like I'm the only one;
Stuck on this Earth,
So lonely my heart just hurt;
Guess I am not a woman's worth,
Got no happiness and mirth;
I'm like an engine that won't start,
Up in your car;
Like inchworms trying to go far,
As little as they are;
Like an eclipse going dark,
So hard to find that spark;
Like a light switch that blew a fuse,
Just bad news;
So descriptive how I feel,
Usually I'm hard like steel;
But got to keep it real,
Lonely right now is how I chill;
So to myself don't know why,
I want to cry.

A Sensual High

See, I met this girl,
Shine like diamonds and pearls;
Hair wrapped in a swirl,
Made my emotions just twist and curl;
She was walking by,
I nodded a hi;
I got so shy,
I stuttered in my sigh;
You know she was fine,
This girl looked on time;
She the type you grind,
She is running all through your mind;
You know that kind,
Got you inventing original lines;
plus you don't know why,
You so hooked to her like it's a high;
She's like a drug,
Everyday that fiend thinking of;
Don't want to mess things up,
Trying to show too much love;
She got me wide open,
This is no joking;
I feel this sensual high,
Like I got knocked by and by;
She knows it, she striking ongoing like daily thunder;
Is she playing now?
Got to really make me wonder.
Stopped her one day this summer,
Asked her for her name and number;
Told her I got this sensual high for her,
It really can't go on any longer.

Too Hard To Heal a Broken Heart

I would never know how to start,
To heal a broken heart;
I don't know about those odds,
I guess you got to hand it over to God;
Maybe you got the right sign,
Maybe that mate was wrong;
You know you must follow your heart and mind,
And pray you get the right one strong;
You do not want your emotions choking,
because you're left all heartbroken;
But then again it is apart of life,
We do things several times
but never cannot get it right;
See, you knew I was going to give it real,
Something so true solid hard like steel;
These are words that will make you feel,
Like love is a tricky gamble still;
and when you got love infected,
You felt a great spice of life;
But when you get heartbroken,
your emotions to LOVE freeze hard like ICE;
And when you try to fall in love
You always think twice;
And you might even create a checklist,
Just make sure everything is real like
white on rice.

My Poetry Got Her SOGGY

Girl like let me blog you this, let me blog you that;
These words will slog you down, you know I am coming off phat;
Poems that get you soggy,
You feel this control on your body;
For you I just meant this to be warm,
I already gave you the warn;
For you I had to jot this down,
I told you that this was shaky ground;
My style can be stunning,
Just go your skin running;
Emotions get into the mood,
I am not trying to run game but the lyric do what it do;
I do not care how the words run,
For the lady keep it sweet like a melted honey bun;
My goal is to get you like a sponge,
Make a mistake calling me, a complete stranger, sweetheart or hun;
Watch who you say those names too;
With your ring on do not forget who is who;
I cannot seem to understand,
How for a second a lady cannot think about her man;
Oh, but that is okay;
My lyrics cannot be used for game play.

Section Fifteen:
LAST MOMENTS

All on Your Last Breath

I could have a cool million,
Or low budget straight chilling;
Sometimes feel so close to death,
Feel like you on your last breath;
Like you got nothing else left,
Plus your health just failed;
You immune system takes on a war,
You don't realize what its for;
Something going on inside,
It's hard to live your life;
It's already hard just to survive,
Then my health just took a dive;
So thankful for every good moment,
The Lord knows I want it;
Blessed to be around,
I got to have faith before my pain will go down;
Feel like a smother,
Like one can't be helped by another;
It's just me and God,
I can't come close to those odds;
I don't deserve my blessings,
Still I learn so many lessons;
God I am thankful yes
If it all happens on my last breath;
So many things can happen,
Just look at how some acting;
So much stress and struggle,
So many ways to get into trouble...

Another Breath

I thank God for another breath,
Even if I got nothing else left;
Thank Him for all my health,
Even if I had wealth;
Just a blessing to see another vision,
Trying to pursue a goal or mission;
Some can't even get into position,
Handicaps block their intentions;
I got another breath to give praise,
Thankful for so many days;
Its like how many more suns will I see?
Blessed if I see one two or three
It's like a got another chance,
In this life I can't freelance;
Life has got in so much desperation,
Another breath looking good on a nation;
You blessed to smile again,
See, so many closest friends;
We got to keep the Lord holy,
I got nothing but Christians who scold me;
I got to just let go,
Walk by the faith of God yo;
Why do I make this hard?
I suppose to fear nothing but God to start;
It's like I got another moment,
It's golden I own it;
I got another time I know I'd want it.

Can You See It All Going Dark

The violence, the car crashing;
Nothing silent, only bad vibes lasting;
The trouble in our schools,
How the television teaches like some teachers do;
The drugs getting out of control,
Gay rights made the poll;
People using planes as weaponry,
I still pray to God set me free;
People dying in any instant gone in a minute;
That second some was on earth last did not see the blessing in it;
Your life like a tunnel width getting tight,
At first was wide like shots on a hockey night;
Can you see it all going dark,
But you got to have that spark;
To push on keep going,
Life keeps on flowing;
You blessed to be five score,
The average is three score and ten years more;
It's hard just living another second,
All this filth got our future going bad like broken records;
But everything happens for a reason, better believe it;
You got to live and receive it.

Every Second Every Breath

Every second every breath, that's all I got left;
Seems like everyday I'm getting closer to death;
Some people keep dying, life is I'm trying to make it;
Praying that my life don't get taken;
But the violent ways never over, murders no closure;
Still trying to live life like I supposed to;
I'm not alone guess it's not my time;
When I go I hope every human felt my rhymes;
Got them all patient, wanting to change the nation;
Make the world into a peaceful situation;
But people got their fate, really go that way;
They really don't know the time or day;
They want to make the best of life everything in it;
You just blessed to be here more than 10 seconds or 10 minutes;
I thank God for every second every breath,
More importantly thank Him for my health;
Every second every breath
God I thank You, when I got nothing left;
I thank you if I got millions,
Or broke chilling.

Last Breath

When the door is about to shut,
And you are miles from your house or hut;
When you have ran only ten minutes,
Still got more to do with no motivation in it;
Like that one rep you cheated on that bench press,
Like that one more problem to push the limits on your stress;
Like that last apology you wanted to make,
But it was too late;
Like that last quick move to make,
But you hesitate;
Like that last nice glimpse of the sky,
But then the horrible weather passes by;
Like that should have, would have, but it came and gone;
Like the chance you had but you took another option it was wrong;
Like only enough energy to go an inch but you need a mile;
Like the finishing touches you needed but could not enhance your
style;
The time has come everything else thereafter TOO LATE
You can't make fate and destiny wait;
You got nothing else,
Left but a last breath.

Section Sixteen:
MATH

BRING ON THE MATH

I got this math thing down,
Could be talk of the town;
Hit me up I will come around,
I am just arithmetic sound;

When it comes to math limits I got no bound,
I am on the trail of the answer like a bloodhound;
Get your answer corrected sit back I am like what now;
Take on hard problems like I guts now;

When it gets tough you know I am the prowl,
Turn a smile from a frown;
Have you sleeping the math wearing it like a gown;
Have you thinking so basic like English predicates and nouns;

I got knowledge by the pound,
My styles go round and round;
You math lost but with me you are found,
Breaking down the math shredded like pepper ground;

So bring on the math it I will surround,
And if I was rusty on prob and stat time to rebound;
With math I got that visual like ultrasound;
My styles profound;

I am so humble to be astounded,
I am just close to next thing like numbers rounded;
See, I just expound;
My character is that of a math circus clown;

To me the hills are like mounds,
The way I break it all down;
Not even famous in this world renown;

Just follow this gift that someone higher than me impound;

So I do not even rhyme for the crown,
Somebody else take it now;
I am just grateful I was able
To make it now, say it break it down;

Time To Intertwine MATH and the Rhyme

See, I mastered it all,
Calculus too basic true;
Even got in some upper level sequences
And some Diff EQ;

Already derived the integration,
Found the Arc length of a curve;
Trying to get people hip to the math
So many thousands already served;

See, I dealt with the vectors
That had direction and length;
Integrated line integrals
That really made me think;

It was all for a purpose,
God has blessed me well;
And still got work to do tutoring math
Always so much more to tell;

I Got Sine and Cosine in my head
And then when off on the Tangent;
And then they got these laws those
Word problems I am strong still standing;

I realized how important functions were
When I got to college;
I was just getting used to factoring
That was something I could acknowledge;

What backs me up
Is when I am in Calculus 2 doing trig;
See, I got learn the subjects well

So I can show up big;

Still got added knowledge to my mind;
It allowed me to be an author years after college this time;
My mind thinking rich could be low budget like having one dime,
But somehow it was time to intertwine the math and the rhyme.

Do the Math and BE HIP

What you thought
I could not do the math and be hip;
I got Calculus to basic down player
So do not even trip;

And yeah if you are falling,
Maybe math teaching is your calling;
Yeah I might not be rich in dollars,
But rich in educating scholars;

See, some taught already white collar,
I made my case I will holler;
But still some will say I am a ghetto geek,
Probably because how I carry myself in a given week;

But I can be hip get emotional in the flow,
You might catch me at the club on my birthday you know;
But I know "y" from "y " prime shake a beat off a rhyme;
And some people say I still got way too much time;

But I do not really care it is my life with these flows strong,
Why would worry about that when time keep moving on;
People still question about my hipness,
How can I be an artist and stay so math gifted;

Styles Uplifted,
Given by the grace of God;
And when it comes to Mercy,
How you compete with those odds;

Yet Math is important in everybody lifeline,
Especially if you are living a life like mine;
And you will know the range,

How much you got to change;

Just to make sure your math is completed,
Don't be hating on math you know you need it;
You might as well get at it be conceited,
It will make you scholarly and you believe it.

Call it Math Knowledge

Come on, you know who this is,
All up in your math biz;
Your success I want to acknowledge,
Let me hit you with some math knowledge;
I know fractions like a half;
I got something to share to get you on the right path;
Everyday you use percent,
Just think about that last sale and how the regular price went;
Do not let sign numbers throw you off,
You already learning that when Tiger Woods wins at golf;
Look at the math all around you,
It's like arithmetic been found you;
You do not even know that you use it,
Math flows in your life like rhythm and music;
You need to know the area of a room,
So things will fit right in soon;
Math is just that tight,
So applied and pure stuck in your life;
You can even predict the next minimum wage,
Look at how we use math these days;
You can even estimate the width of
Hurricane Ike's eyes yes,
Math can be just an educated guess.

You Know Who to Call From Calculus to Basic

I got that math down from Calculus to basic,
Math is like life it is a challenge plus we face it;
And you know we always trying to get to the answer,
And we need to have the steps down like disco club dancers;
And knowledge is power and I know this is certain,
We need obstacles to make us clever or we as a nation just hurting;
And math and science looking like the cornerstone;
We living in a technological world, so get your skills bring them on;
Believe it or not you can see calculus as math basic,
You just need the confidence to go get it chase it;
And when you get the knowledge you feel good and grace it,
You just needed the faith and if you got it just embrace it;
And your mind like boiling water cooking,
Others shocked at how you looking;
Do not get bigheaded and get so took,
Just remember God allowed you the knowledge that got you so shook;
I am just a supporter in your successful path,
You can feed off of me I am just another parasite infecting you with the knowledge of math.

YOU KNOW ME MR. MATH and RHYMES

This style you cannot hate it,
So motivated;
I am trying to give out the math knowledge,
Still just another success story from college;
Math skills flow like the dirty Mississippi,
Yet I am down for success get on the bandwagon if you with me;
I salute basic math, college algebra, and even trig;
But I challenge calculus, and upper levels so I like to do it big;
But who do you know talk about the math and rhyme;
Still so critical in life at the same time;
You blessed you even got another chance to be educated,
Some could not make it to this day you know I hate it;
I am just a parasite for teaching the math,
Do it up so cool just to see who I am reaching with the math;
Say a rhyme,
Like you love it at the time,
Thankful if I am still breathing,
Teaching college students and they are receiving;
I thank God for the blessing,
Yet I still learn many lessons.

Where My Math Soldiers At?

Where my math soldiers at?
Trying to keep you right on path;
Coming off just like that,
Rhyming about the math;
And I do it calculus to basic,
It's a math world let us face it;
This real life it is not funny,
Kind of messed up when you do not know
twenty percent of your own money;
But my math soldiers locked into position,
They look like geniuses and scholars
but we no have no prideful intentions;
And some said I was the lieutenant, but I am not worthy;
But still in it to win it, but God had allowed me to serve thee;
And I give out the knowledge;
I gained right from college;
I thank God for the blessing,
Been through so many lessons.

Mr. Math Tutor

It is so true,
I'm getting noticed in my city too;
Most say I'm that math genius,
But they don't really mean it;
They say I'm the perfect suitor,
MR. MATH TUTOR;
Flush out your math fear, like plumbers with Roto Rooter;
Touch the fractions like HALF,
Just to get you on the right path;
I got to get you hip with this math,
You flow with the numbers cleansed fresh like you just had a bath;
I keep you all but stuck,
Some say I talk in riddles too much;
I do that and more I bring the knowledge all and such;
I do this all the time,
Just math and rhyme;
You got to know my kind,
It can't be short of fine;
I'm just the right aid,
To keep you with grade A;
I'm not even thinking about satisfied C,
I am always thinking at the highest level when I achieve;
I thank God for my knowledge,
I thank him for getting me through college;
He allowed me to this math,
Now I got to help people in their path.

Section Seventeen:
FOR THE LADY

SAY WHAT IS UP WITH THIS LADY

Say what is up with this lady
Got me going crazy in my mind;
Looking so good every inch every curve
In her clothes so fine;

And maybe it is the strut in the way she walks,
And maybe it is how she moves her butt or the sweetness in her
talk;
For her I would write many flows just to see that sweet candy drop
smile,
And if she is spiritual and intellectual she got me going wild;

It is like she passed my application
Everything just checks out smooth;
Now I must come with sugar and spice
Correct with all my moves;

See, once you got a lady's heart
It is hard for her to let go;
And she might help take the weight off those boulders
In your episodes;

Nothing like a lady's touch,
A Man loves when it is like Charmin smooth;
She is looking so hot like a heater,
And I am like a fan to her we so cool.

Can I Breathe Your Breathe?

Girl Can I breathe your breathe?
Give you what you need;
Make you feel real soft,
Not trying to get you off;
Just want to be your friend,
Go on dates again and again;
We have some fun just smooching,
That's what I like doing;
Enjoy life with a smile,
I'm hooked up with your style;
Everything too nice now,
It's going down;
Maybe later go steady,
Right now just not ready;
Got it on hold like on the phone dial,
Let's take it slow awhile;
I just want you by my side,
When I'm having a good time at night;
We go good together tight,
Everything so alright;
I just wanted to breathe your breath,
Get you what you need;
Together we can walk our walk,
As a couple we talk the talk;
We like two peas in a pot,
Things get a little hot;
But this part is so golden,
This moment we holding;
I'm breathing your breath you breathing my breath,
We so good together don't you see.

Can My Words Get You Feeling Good

Girl you like sugary icing on a dry cake;
When you support the many moves I make;
Even though I come hard like steel,
Soft is how you make me feel,
I know it's real;
Look at your confidence,
Mine came gone just went;
But your beauty I'm still pondering,
I'm wandering;
Girl just look at what you do,
Got me creating good feeling words for you;
You got my heart like a door all open,
My heart slogging and soaking;
I don't know what it's going to take,
To make you feel good anyway;
You already too confident in the play,
Hope you say its okay;
I'm just saying what's on my mind,
My heart flow the grind;
I like the style of your kind,
Women like you so hard to find;
I'm still complimenting
You aren't even flinching;
There's so much I got to mention,
And begging is not my intention;
I want to make you feel good;
Not like you normally would.

Cannot Call It A Relationship

I had known this girl for some time,
But I thought we would be talking
but she wants to be the friendly kind;
But she got me sugar-coated,
I was like wait a minute hold it;
I am thinking something exploding,
But she keep switching modes and;
This is no doubt,
I was just trying out to figure her out;
She said we could talk,
But never walked the walk;
She treated me like fries,
I wanted to be her main porterhouse surprise;
What is wrong with this situation here?
I cannot call it a relationship;
If I really thought about it I would say,
This is closer to game play;
This thing we got is not strong,
It's like a light switching off and on;
I hope we do not blow a fuse,
Yet it seems that I am already having the blues;
It was like she had me on this long business hold;
Like I should wait for her down the road,
Cannot call this a relationship.

Three-Fourths of My Heart (2007)

Lady I am sorry, but this time Roses I refuse to give;
Once again I am sorry, but it is not enough to apologize still;
Lady I am sorry, I cannot give you my mind;
Because I need it to think about how to keep you at this time;
I cannot give you my body, for me that is not how to start;
My emotions seem so delicate to me
So I will give three-fourths of my heart;
And my feelings keep screaming your name,
So locked on you so tight;
Now I feel so soft so loosed in your right;
And the other one-fourth connects up with my mind,
And that is how I came up with these nice words so fine;
My apology is complete now she knows,
I just want to be next to her heart
So we can help each other grow.

Section Eighteen:
MISCELLANEOUS

What If Every Line Came Out In Rhyme

What if every line,
Came out your mouth in rhyme;
You know the freestyle kind,
It is fueled in your mind;
You get all amped up got the juices flowing,
There really is no stopping you so you just keep on going;
People just shocked how you are spitting,
And they cannot be mad because it is the truth they are getting;
Serving up people just look at how you deliver,
Your flow could be clean or dirty bad like the Mississippi River;
It is just spoken word, not to be evil or up surd;
It might be the truth and that has to be heard;
And you could call me ghetto geek because I am smart from the
hood;
I just write about real life experiences some can be no good;
I am not a fan of the negative vibes,
I am clearly rhyming to get the word out and help lives;
I keep the flow smooth still,
I talk about everything in rhyme I got this vision that I feel.

I Keep Poems Storming

I keep poems storming,
It could be early in the morning;
Rhyme dangerous words without warning,
It's real knowledge that is alarming;
talk about the world more,
I have to come with similes and metaphors;
In life so many adventures so much to explore,
So many struggles now you see who I am writing for;
It's like I am writing back to myself expressions uplifted,
I would not say that I am prideful,
But some say I am gifted;
I must keep the lyric smooth,
Like the body of a baby some people know what I can do;
Make the poem warm yes,
Still a broken vessel almost always I must confess;
I just write whatever is on my mind,
And the truth hurts and it can be hard to find;
But write I write it all tell in rhyme,
I think of new lyrics in every second of time.

Unique Poet

Anybody know it,
I am that unique poet;
Dropping fresh similes and metaphors,
The people know what I am headed for;
Spoken word I just spit it,
People just thought I just rhyme but to writing I am committed;
And you should not forget it,
If you want my style come and get it;
You know you down and with it,
Stop hating just quit it;
I could come with fables,
The good and bad like Cain and Abel;
Run the style and plan across your table;
But you thinking I am not able;
I told you I was that unique poet,
Some critics just know it,
These rhymes I do not flow them,
These styles I just show them;
See, some people will never understand,
The vision I carry with a pen and pad in my hand.

Think About What Peace Means (May 2008)

See, you better watch what you doing being violent to your brother,
Because that man was probably someone
That was supposed to help your grandmother;
See, why be violent and put your mind through that ordeal;
And you might be after a good person,
That supposed to help you later on in your life still;
See, you never know what will happen in your life design;
And everybody has his or her road because I surely got mine;
This is why we must show the love, yet so many gone astray;
We need a worldwide peace call
Because some was brought up the wrong way;
And some people make some mistakes
Because that was how they were raised,
But if my heart is still beating
I thank God for mercy and praise.

My Thoughts Runneth Over

So many layoffs,
It's no payoff;
Feels like I am doing hard time,
On this part-time;
Yet I am so unique,
In most words I speak;
My mind strong and stout like shoulders,
My thoughts just runneth over;
Look at how I'm acting,
Predicting what might happen;
Stressed-out vibes keep stacking,
Feels like I'm burning like how meat blackened;
What's going on inside,
I mean what's really in my mind;
All these future thoughts overflowing,
But I dream I'm not knowing;
I think about these visions,
That comes to prove points like fables on television;
They got me questioning my decision,
Forgetting my mind intentions;
My thoughts pile like files stacked,
Good or bad I can't control how they act;
As a matter of fact,
I'm confused on what's appropriate or exact;
My thoughts run over,
I try to stay righteous sober;
I need a crying shoulder,
Blessed if I get older.

Section Nineteen:
FAITH

Going Thru the Rain

Trust in God to take you thru the storm,
That caused you so much pain;
He will keep your heart healed and warned,
So that you will not drive yourself insane;

See, it must be his reason,
If you are left here still breathing;
See, you never know what age you are reaching,
I am just saying what I think is real not preaching;

But times keep changing,
I got this vision I totally see;
But I have no control of the motives
That is really beyond me;

I cannot move on my own strength,
When situations get tough;
See, everybody faces some rain,
Degrees of pain can be brutal tough;

But if God kept you still breathing,
I thought I said it was for His reason;
See, in you He has a purpose,
I know somebody heard this;

And we make so many mistakes,
And we never see the full picture;
Never even thought about how God
Wants to use you and get you.
We got so many lessons to learn,
So much of life to live on thru;
Even though I write these nice lines
I am still nowhere near perfect too;

But everybody has a little rain,
And you need God to bear it thru;
Because something could hit you so hard,
Like it knocked you into oblivion too;

But I must push on,
Because my heart is yet still beating;
See, everybody has their number,
If I am alive mercy is the reason;

See, if I made it another morning,
Some people go without a warning,
See, some people are blind and cannot see;
Probably concentrate on faith way better than me;

So much some take for granted,
Why am I trying to compare;
God put me here for a unique reason,
What matters is how He cares;

And some storms I go thru,
Allows me to build up stronger;
See, you gain a little wisdom;
Because you hold resistance longer;

That rain seem like pain,
Weakened my shoulders;
But I must pick my head up stronger
Because if I breathe my life is not over;

See, in every breath there is joy,
Live life, have fun enjoy;
Because time never stands still,
But aren't you glad that rain never hung around for real;

See, the sunshine is on the way,
The hope for a better day;
But nobody said times would be perfect,
And Christians would tell you that grace, we do not deserve it;

I will be glad if I ever get through the rain,
That nearly drove me insane;
And this is why I need God
Intercepting my heart and brain.

FAITH with FINANCE and FINDING a MATE

See, if God gave me another breath
I was spared mercy;

And if I believe in God I must have faith
Even in tough times you heard me;

So many people living worse,
Why should I go insane?

Thankful if I still got my legs arms and feet
And I can survive with a clever brain;

And one can have the faith, mercy
wisdom, hope, knowledge, and many more like those there of;

But even in these tough times
The greatest virtue is that of love;

See, the ending of chaotic ways
Is where love starts.

See, when you help somebody,
It really feels good on your heart;

What I cannot understand,
Is why the poor have to help the poor;

You would think billionaires would
Just help out a little bit more;

And this even affects my living
I fear choices I make will be wrong;

Some people already make some money,
And they sing some sad song;

But was it really faith in God or just a
Stupid decision you made;

But the only way you can resolve this
Is to take it to the Lord in pray;

So I drop to my knees,
Say God I thank You I know I had some wrongs now;

But if You left me still breathing
I must say hallelujah and praise and worship You anyhow;

See, some people did not make it
To this second in time;

But Glory to God I was
Able to finish another rhyme;

We must have some faith
Like the move is already done;

And we leave the baggage for God
He allows us to work for His Glory and fun;

See, it was never about me,
This is not even my shine;

Some moves I might have made in this life
But it was already known by the Divine;

But I must have faith
And hope is on the way you know;

Still cannot wait to see
That gold on the other end of the rainbow;

Even in these times,
Hard to want to date a lady and get married soon;

The lady wants kids in a hurry,
But the man wants to take it slow like a smooth tune;

Now food and shelter matter
Especially when you barely have a job strong;

I will never blame God for this economic mess
This is a man made issue that has been carried on;

But I still have hope!!!

FAITH IN GOD MUST BE STRONG

I made it past two storms
But another is around the way;
And what if you got to hold out
And it is no time to evacuate;

And then in the winter you catch a cold,
And the weather takes you under;
It feels there is a bothersome gnat in your episodes
But you must hold resistance longer;

See, faith is like foundation brick,
So you cannot be hoping for sand;
Because when a hurricane comes
You cannot rebuild
because washed away is your land;

And my finances just slipping
But then again I never have to worry;
And I must pray to God for the right answer
Because I know in my heart He is worthy;

And disasters could drive you insane,
But at least God left your heart beating;
You cannot set your mind on material things,
Because you will leave those upon retreating.

And really it does not matter
If things should go wrong;
Peace and Love should just scatter
And we all must have the faith to stay strong.

Faith Rocks

It's like hard and firm,
Fight off the germ;
Like algae that kept clinging,
But this did not do a thing and;
Its got all this courage,
its purpose is to service;
And be strong like forceful winds,
Its power I can transcend;
It takes on all complication,
It knows how to handle every situation;
It's like a rock taking damage,
It's burning hot but it can stand it;
You question where is the fear and coward,
But it sustained so much power;
Like a rock that went through a war,
But yet it could take some more;
Wish I had this courage sober,
My worries would be over;
It's embedded in a five-letter word;
Comes from the God I am supposed to serve;
Wish I could be that rock,
Anticipating everything and what not;
Wish I could take a beating,
And then things got more heated;
Look at such confidence to press on,
No stress ever to hold you wrong;
Faith keeps you strong,
Living life-long.
FAITH ROCKS

Faith Comes in Many Flavors

We cannot control what faith we will get,
Or how it will even hit;
Faith is not easy to attain,
Not having it will drive you insane;
It comes in so many flavors,
Goes with your behavior;
The best is by way of the Holy Spirit,
You feel good when you hear it;
Then there is physical faith,
That gets your body parts straight;
Then there is the mind it gets mental,
Faith feel used like time from a car rental;
There is emotional faith that keeps you feeling glad,
You keep that courage through strong events good or bad;
There's nothing like spiritual faith,
Its takes patience like a hospital room wait;
Having faith is not being a coward,
You feel good in that hour;
But it was not your faith that made things right,
Its was your work through God's might;
Faith comes in many types,
When you accomplish the task you are hype;
Faith I never own it,
That is God in that moment;
That shines His Glory,
Before me.

Felt Like My Life Was Drowning

I needed to gasp for life,
Cause nothing went right;
I lost a twenty last week,
My voice went hoarse I couldn't speak;
I got boils on my back,
Like I had an allergic attack;
I'm going insane,
I can't bare the pain;
I'm glad I can still breathe,
Visually see; hear like canines smell,
Feels like I still go through hell;
My sinuses out of control,
Benadryl couldn't put my problem on hold;
So many personal problems amounting,
Feel like my life was drowning;
Like I had no life raft,
I just had to have faith to continue the path;
Hope things got better,
Everything got back together;
Like time was the cover,
My life felt so smothered;
Just thankful for all the good moments,
Jesus knows I'd want it;
I had so many bad situations,
It's still hard to live even with an occupation;
Its just things I want, but I grab what I need; feels like suffocation,
But I survive I'm patient.

I Got to Forget and Move On

Someone close to me died,
I got to let it ride;
If I let it bog me down,
My lifestyle looking suicide;
So many trials and tribulations,
To interrupt a changing nation
We got to keep on pacing,
Or time is wasting;
Cannot relive the past,
Cause it never last;
The present is this moment,
It's golden you own it;
If you wanted to make a change,
It comes with pain;
My life cannot suffer,
Because of the death of another;
We all got our day all sisters and brothers;
Some people go earlier then others;
Wish the whole world let peace and love smother;
No matter how close,
People just ghost;
And if I don't move on, my will for life will be wrong;
Soon or later my life will sing the death song;
We cannot live infinity long, what's done will be done;
We could go off this planet old or young;
We got to forget keep moving,
Be righteous in what we are doing.

Section Twenty:
God Help The World
(January 2009 version)

God Help The World (Part 1)

What happened to the economic cycle?
Many years ago things were actually running smooth;
But every since gas prices rose,
Bad times happen in big moves;

And someone might be greedy
Someone might be holding on to cash;
But there are less rich and poor people
How long will this economy destruction last?

And job security looking lost,
This can mess with human feelings strong;
But Glory to God if I am alive though still cheap
But breathing and moving along;

And why should I spend my money?
And get in more debt than I can handle;
This economic downturn seems like
A tricky game or scandal;

You almost have to hustle,
Or invent something people can really use;
You try to work entry-level at a job,
Then a year later you get a severance package and bad news;

But I must be grateful if I'm still walking
Because some cannot do that for real;
And worse of all I am living
With out health insurance still;

If rich people are on edge,
How you think the poor feel?
You have to know I will not be big spending,

You can call me cheap, broke; it is about survival for real;

And change is going to come,
The hope of a better tomorrow;
Tired of hearing about layoffs everyday,
So many people left in sorrow.

God have mercy help the world

God Help The World (Part 2)

It is already enough drama
Just surviving in the 'hood;
And then you have this terrible economy,
Not running the way it should;

And banks buying out others,
And the housing market gone astray;
My, my, my God,
I just pray for some better days;

Consumer confidence gone down the drain,
The blessings of small businesses lost;
And too many people seem greedy,
But look at how much trouble it cost;

And people already stressed out,
Holding onto their last leg for real;
But thank goodness God get the glory
In every single ordeal;

But struggles just happen
Mercy was spared to handle things for real;
See, one cranium is worth nothing,
But multiple brains can storm a great thing still;

See, why did the gas have to rise,
And make people spend all they had;
See, that is why the mortgage crisis happened
And that is so sad;

And when the stocks keep crashing,
More layoffs follow;
And job security now

Looking more hollow;

But I pray God helps us,
Only you know the source of the answer now;
Just give me the right road,
And guide me that way anyhow.

God Help The World (Part 3)

So many issues can happen
With a struggling economy still;
See, God already supplied the mercy
I give praise it is not chaotic for real;

See, times could be really worst,
So hard to get the job you want still;
You just hope the job you have is recession-proof,
But that is even a risk for real;

And you cannot be too careful,
Because storms come without warning;
But then again someone probably died
Younger than me and I am blessed to see another morning;

See, some people are just suffering,
Some people have real pain they can feel;
You might not have a job
But at least you got your limbs still;

You got to thank God for the simple,
Thank Him for the challenges yes;
And recognize through it all,
That God still blesses;

See, if God left me still breathing
He had a purpose in mind;
And I may never know it,
But I pray for some direction this time;

So many things could happen,
And then your book is a closed chapter;
I used to think "GET MONEY"

But now survival for Christ is what I am after;

And I had to say this
This goes out to every man, woman, boy and girl;
So many trials and tribulations to face,
God please help the world.

God Help The World (Part 4)

You got to be thinking careful now,
But you cannot be too careful enough;
Food borne illnesses can happen,
And the economy is bad, making it rough;

You cannot even ask why,
You got to be blessed if you are even alive;
Because any move is a risk in your life;
Whether you fly, walk, or drive;

But God already supplied the mercy,
Our chapters are already written in stone;
Even with a terrible economy,
Love keeps pushing things moving along;

We might have war overseas,
But we have wars in our neighborhoods streets;
Yet it seems more violence happen
The greater we keep preaching peace;

God help us in all areas,
Purify and nurture the land;
I'll admit I have not been the best I can be,
If You have these trials in place I understand;

But I know that You love me,
But it has been days that You spared me so;
And if I am still breathing another moment,
I must give You praise in this flow;

So many obstacles to face,
So many bumps in my road;
You really must have faith in God

To carry your cross through some episodes;

See, if you are used to the hurricane,
You already know how the storm goes;
See, that is wisdom in your life,
Because what matters is what is worse in our lives you know;

God Help the World

God Help The World (Part 5)

People talk about a recession,
But we need a revival strong;
So people's confidence about job security,
Can get back to normal and carry on;

Somebody out there is greedy,
And we have many others who need it;
And while some people lives tumble,
And some already had their number;

Be blessed for another day,
If you still have all your limbs;
Because that might not be the situation,
For the next her or him;

Some people are born that way,
Some come deaf or blind;
But Glory to God for my deficiencies
They keep me humble for him at this time;

God please help the world,
I know you got an answer I can feel;
I know Your moves will come with faith and grace
Genuine and harder than fine steel;

I believe there is always hope,
But I know things can get worse;
But all these tribulations are more reason enough
To always keep You in my mind first;

So many thoughts in my head,
So many blessings already achieved;
I am even blessed right this moment,

If I am alive and I can still breathe;

And I cannot wait for that summer joy,
Because his Mercy spared me strong;
I might have a year long cold,
But I know God can help the world and pull everything along;

Be blessed!

Section Twenty-One:
DEAR GRANNY

Dear Granny 1

See, her Bible's may be old and shabby,
Dear Granny, thanks for wisdom, you always make me happy;
You the one told me to have faith through the mission,
Keep pressing on live life in my position;
Make the right moves because God always there for me,
I know two people in the world God and you cared for me;
See, I remember how you raised me,
Taught me how to be respectful to the ladies;
You showed me so much,
I wish I could take it all but I cannot get enough;
Always told me that Jesus and that dollar are your true friends,
Always keep up in prayer and smile live life to the end;
Keep your head right to stay out of the cellblocks,
And work hard, be grateful when that check hit the mailbox;
And you used to teach me my timetables and taught me the rules,
Even took a switch to my backside if I could not tie my own shoes;
Because of God through you I got the courage,
You told me have faith with God you cannot be nervous;
Dear Granny, I'll love you forever.

Dear Granny 2

Granny, I remember when you were calling my name,
When the streetlights went on and I was with friends
As we were ending our game;
It was Hide and Seek on the street yeah that is right,
Catch a Girl, Get a Girl, and all that jive;
but those days we really had fun,
Kids got lost in the street and parents did not worry about a gun;
Remember shows that only told morals and fables,
Then we would act what we saw and it improved our behavior;
Lady, you know we had some rough times,
Getting caught up by the police a couple of times;
Then mom was up to no good,
Still listened to my granny her voice never faded in the hood';
Never ran with a gang or participated in a clubhouse,
Only found love in granny she gave much love out;
She had been around at least eighty years,
Faced all the fears;
Now she shed ancient tears, I
still appreciate her and she's still here;
Dear Granny, I love you my dear

Dear Granny 3

As I got older I started rhyming and did the math;
One I took in as a hobby the other I tried to master its path;
And math became the subject I would teach,
Did not realize how many people I have already reached;
I kept on rhyming even though some of it did not make sense,
I was afraid some might not like it so I got tense;
Now I got many rhymes that's already done, I cannot remember
them all;
And Granny you always asked me about the poetry awards on the
wall;
And you knew I was just addicted to math knowledge,
Still thankful you were able to see me get a master from college;
I know you're proud I cannot thank you enough,
I know God was in this plan, it was really tough;
Even though I was beat by a man who was not my dad,
Granny made sure we got through the times,
It does not matter good or bad;
I cannot hate it, because
My Granny, you are appreciated.

Dear Granny 4

Hey Granny you been there since day one;
And you would pop me with the extension cord
If I got slick in my fun;
You were working hard to keep us acting right,
Yet some neighbors saw my success
And they got surprised;
Granny you helped me to finish school,
Even told me I would be successful too;
Too bad I never had the same faith,
But I still think God works on me today;
Some things I just feel I will never understand,
But you told me I couldn't analyze everything in this land;
But you always knew I hate taking risks,
Yet you always say put God in up in the mix;
I remember those scary nights I had sweaty palms,
But you made me sit down and read
The Twenty-Third Psalms;
I thought I might lose it, because I was scared for me
No matter what times we had, at least you cared for me;
And then we had been through some wicked times,
But we laugh and giggled and kicked it fine..

Dear Granny 5

I thank God again for the blessings,
For my Granny too who has been here over 80 years
She has taught many so much about life's learned lessons;
No matter how old, you never really lose it,
Like some people do in rap music;
You thought about my heart as a kid,
I cannot put a price on how much you did;
I just cherish the memory,
I just wish we could be together to infinity;
Right now I know I am not doing so bad,
But I could do better just to make you glad;
All grown up now it's like we best friends,
You might see me hit 40 but that all depends;
But with you I think I have had the best life,
Did it without the force of a father, dad yes that is right;
Although I really wish I could understand,
How to fix things like every modern man;
But you still taught me about the softer side,
I thank God for that and the brighter side;
You told me to treat the ladies with all respect,
Never to call them out their names, no none of that,
DEAR GRANNY, you have my deepest respect.

Section Twenty-Two:
Loose Ends

Thankful If I Still I Breathe

See, if I made it another morning,
Some gone without a warning;
Sickness set in weighed heavy,
Still got this cough going steady,

I got boils on my body,
And what if I really had no job;
I would be worthless to a hottie;
Feeling like my life was robbed;

And I had just lost some money,
This part is real not funny;
In this terrible economy that is sad,
I cared about that dollar man I am so mad;

Instances in my life kept going wrong,
But then I heard this news someone passed away gone;
And my day keeps going worst,
But I think about the fact if I am still breathing first;

And the next day cometh,
And then I awake with a refreshed smile;
And I am so glad for another day,
I get to enjoy it awhile;

See, I could have been sick.
But someone is going thru worst;
I just had to have hope
That times would get better not worse;

And during my shine the rain begin to fall,
But I was so glad he warned me about the wet weather and all;
And later I was feeling better,

And my day got back together;

See, I was doing all this complaining,
But really I was not receiving;
The fact I was not too bad if
My mind and heart was going I was still breathing;

See, some people cannot even struggle,
Some people really cannot begin to run;
See, someone is always doing worse,
And everybody has issues and cannot get things done;

But be grateful if you can still breathe

Just Call Me Clever

Some call me a lyricist,
Some call me a poet;
Some will say I am rapper
I already know it;

These styles I just flow it,
My way I go with;
If you trying to hate you cannot hold it,
Guess what, my vibe just exploded;

Hear I go again,
Another book 2010,
I try to write for the times we are in,
I got pages and pages of rhymes my friend;

See, I write for the rhyme,
Don't mind making them dollars;
Make use of my lifeline;
Some fine ladies give me a holler;

I got the plan underway,
Thought in the past about this day;
Getting people so took,
Stuck all my rhymes in a book;

Words strike like thunder,
Kind of make you wonder;
How I can do the math,
Teach calculus and make you laugh;

Write the Science Fiction that strike like storms,
Ladies read it sweetened like a charm;
And I got the plot so stinky like

Three-day-old underarms;

Be alarmed how I drop it,
On any topic;
Because once you get me started
I just cannot stop it;

See, I will make sure
The critics will approach me never;
They might say I am not poetically pure
But I hope they call me clever.

With God, All You Can DO Is Wonder

See, struggles be weight like boulders,
Like your life is close to over;
I know someone heard me,
But then you like Lord have MERCY;

You so mad one day in your race,
Just kept doing your thing never thought about GRACE;
You are trying to keep everything straight,
But really is it all about your own personal FAITH;

You are so great with the WISDOM,
Fronting like you had it for years;
But really someone passed you the torch
When you and that person shared past tears;

And you got the courage to face your fears,
But LOVE can be a tricky game you need God's ear to hear;
See, really God I can truthfully TRUST,
I would rather tithe all my funds than to give into continuous lust;

Within myself, always, trying to find ultimate PEACE,
But when I pray and rejoice that is my release;
And then when I was HUMBLE, BLESSINGS overflowing,
So many of them coming at me I need to pray which direction I am
going;

And when I had too much pride,
I was just so blind to see;
How much more
God really had in store for me,

And when I became more PATIENT,
The future rewards set in place;

And as I got more Bible Knowledge
In my soul my fear about certain things was erased;

See with God,
All you really can do is wonder;
The gracious moves he already got in place,
Untold positions never to take you under.

TIME MOVES ON

Time moves on, the past already faded;
You knew things would not last, it was anticipated;
So why stress yourself about drama,
that pause you like commas;

When you should really halt with an exclamation,
Like what is happening after your living situation;
See, time waits for no soldier,
You better enjoy every bit of your life before it is over;

See. I hate being bored, glad to see another morn;
See, some got stuff, cannot take it any more, I just smile and move
on;
See God had allowed many sins yeah we do this,
Some we even committed and do not act like I am the only that do
it;

And we are so blessed time moves on,
Hate to keep reliving the bad;
See, those kinds of memories need to be
Left in the past;

Even though God's Word never changed,
The ways of this world cannot stay the same;
See, we need God in these desperate times,
See, I will always need him every millisecond of my lifeline;

See, God's mercy is more than that guy did wrong in that electric
chair and,
That grace over time passed where I can respect the air and;
You know about those incidents long gone you recollect and stare
and;
You know this physical life is but a light glare and

I want the clock to move faster but at times I want time to be like
the tortoise and I am the hare and,
Some consequences in life you must deal with cannot really care
and;
Time keeps moving on it does not matter whether you are here or
there and;
I know you want good things to last long and it does not and you
like Hey, this is not fair and;

You never looking at the fact you blessed if you can still breathe
and,
You already took life for granted but you caught up now who you
going to receive in;
You living this physical life fleshly ways but be sure to know who
you believe in,
We all make mistakes in our lives and get wake up calls where we
need him.

Section Twenty-Three:
Everything Should End With
LOVE

I Know Someone Who Loves Me

See, God hates some of my ways,
I can admit to that so;
Because I said they were my ways
Not the way He wanted them to go;

And I will suffer the trouble,
Just because I did not hear;
And some stuff I put myself through
I shed so many tears;

But then I count it all as mercy and blessings
Learned so many lessons;
Still want to be more knowledgeable
For what God wants it's worth his essence;

I wish I had the wisdom,
See, my heart, mind and soul not worth it;
See, I need to pray because I am not perfect;

See, I thought about the curvy, bumpy path,
But God knows way past the straight one;
I am still trying to do the math,
Figure I need so many roads but he figure you can just take one;

See, when I get into accidental trouble,
In Spirit, I should really never get lost;
See, there is no other sacrifice than what
Jesus gave up for us on that cross;

See, even if no one else will love me,
I know He is above me;
I know someone that loves me,
I know He really thinks of me;

See, Jesus is really all I need,
I know He loves me;
All I got to do is trust in Him, and His will and believe.

Love Is A Common Cold

Love can come and go,
Or stick around like a disease;
Interrupt your ordinary flow,
For a bigger plan at ease;
You are in a lovesick puppy stance,
You try to fight it but cannot so you drop your hands;
And it hangs on you for a while,
Like a crush gone out of style;
But you could be in love right now,
Your emotions just go wild;
At one point you might not feel remorse,
But then you are back on course;
Trying to get it out of you is no cure,
Because the way you feel is natural and pure;
And your body cannot let it go;
It will not accept any other flow;
Try to take your mind off things to heal,
But you still got this same feel;
Tried to ignore this thing,
But your hormones just go boomerang,
You cannot tell when it is gone,
If it leaves, it's on its own.

Love Looking Like A Drug

Love might as well be a drug,
If you are living for God's will;
I would rather be a fiend for Christ,
Than to be slave to sin for real;
And sometimes you can give your all
And miraculous blessings come your way;
And even if you should fall,
God will come if you call
Strong arms to pick you back up
And then you back in the race;
so do not give up on love; some people say it is a scary road;
But if you have come along way with someone,
Why would you get someone new to explore;
See we really cannot understand love,
It is one of those you cannot lay a hand on for real;
And that is why it is an element that is important
With faith, mercy, grace, and hope still.

Love Manipulator

This lady trying to make me feel soft,
Loves the way I get off;
Loves my personality and attitude,
Just love all my analytical moves;
And she approached me like cotton candy sweet;
So smooth just for me,
she will roll the red carpet out,
She will find ways to keep me no doubt;
And you know she is going that extra inch and a mile;
She is trying to manipulate me to be attracted to her style;
And she will try all she can since she likes the way I glow;
And she is a love manipulator, and will find a way for me to go;
And she will have it made so comfortable and smooth;
This is some kind of lady so undercover with hers too.

True Love Who Can Know When It Comes (Feb 2008)

You cannot tell when true love hit you,
Only God can know;
And you do not have to investigate the purpose,
Because it will surely show;

See, when too starving hearts come together,
Harmonious love intertwines;
You will go thru some struggle
But it will be better if you recognize
you go together like steak and expensive wine;

True love hit you like a slow gentle touch,
This is not lust you must understand;
This is so much bigger beyond
Emotional passion in a fleshy stance;

See, I cannot describe it,
Because it is like a match made in Heaven smooth;
It is like an axiom I cannot derive it,
True love is what it is and that is how it do...

What Is Up About This Thing Called Love

See, when you ride that thing called love
It is like a roller coaster for real;
You know what I am thinking of,
Because even living single have its ups and downs still;

And when love caught your emotion
You felt this beautiful change;
And you start working on the new motions,
Because you must share your life in the game;

But I am really here to tell you,
The love of God will never fail you;
Blessed if He allowed me another day to breathe,
The nation is going thru incidents bigger than humans can see;

I hope God put your LOVE together,
Because that will always work still;
And even thru the wicked disasters
Your foundation is sturdy and real;

So what's up with this thing called love?
But really you might be thinking of lust;
True love is golden sure enough,
And the wicked vibes you cannot ever trust!

Other Books by Author

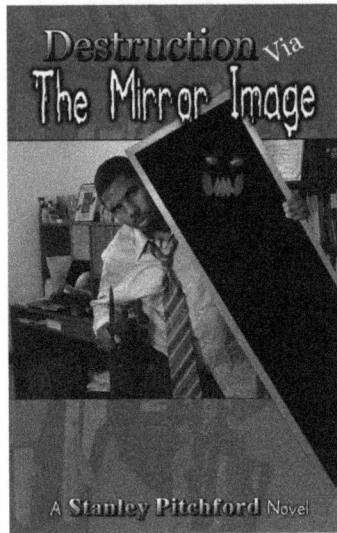

Destruction Via the Mirror Image - Stanley Pitchford's book is about twelve astronauts picked to explore outer space in hopes of finding a discovery interesting to mankind. Once in space, they encounter a creature on the ship. This creature is so hard to figure out that they must find the monster's weakness in order to destroy it. On this space exploration, lives are sacrificed, passion and romance erupts while blackmail attempts surface.

Author Stanley Pitchford weaves an interesting and unique science fiction novel that explores outer space and shows what can happen when we attempt to address the unknown universe

http://www.prioritybooks.com

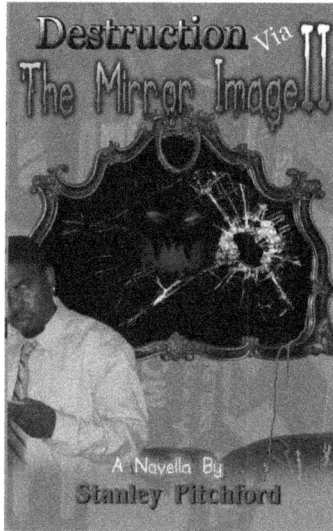

"Destruction via The Mirror Image II - Stanley Pitchford, More Years Later," focuses on several astronauts who attempt to explore outer space, but are joined by an unwelcomed creature that must be annihilated. Tune in as this horrific creature attempts to tragically destroy each astronaut's life for the sake of creating offspring through its victims' dead bodies.

Once again, Stanley Pitchford weaves an interesting and unique science fiction novel that explores outer space and shows what can happen when we attempt to address the unknown universe.

http://www.prioritybooks.com